현대 영미시의 이해

작가별로 읽기

최동오 편저

신아사

책머리에

이 책은 학생들이 현대 영미시를 작가별로 읽고 이해하기 위해 준비되었다. 그러므로 작가와 작품의 선택에는 편역자의 선호가 가장 크게 반영되었음을 밝힌다. 특히 더피(Duffy)와 스나이더(Snyder)가 그렇다. 이 두 작가는 여전히 그 대표성과 예술성을 검증받고 있는 중이라 생각된다.

번역은 동국대학교 출판부에서 낸 이창배의『현대영미시 감상 I』와『현대영미시 감상 II』, 그리고 탐구당에서 출판한 이재호의『20세기 영시』와 이영걸의『20세기 미시』를 많이 참조했다. 또 연구논문 데이터베이스인 KISS(Koreanstudies Information Service System)에 등록된 개별 시인들에 대한 연구논문도 많이 참조했다. 하지만 모든 번역은 최종적으로 내 검토 하에 실렸음을 밝힌다. 번역은 대단히 어려운 작업이다. 기존의 번역물이 나오게 힘을 쏟은 많은 분에게 존경을 표하고 싶다.

시인들에 대한 간략한 소개는 대개 인터넷 사이트인 Academy of American Poets (poets.org)에서 뽑았다. 보충 설명이 필요한 경우 인터넷 사이트인 Poetry Foundation (www.poetryfoundation.org)과 W. Jackson Bate와 David Perkins가 1986년에 편집한 *British & American Poets: Chaucer to the Present*(San Diego: Harcourt)를 참조했다.

개별 시는 아래 시집들에서 가져왔으며 위의 인터넷 사이트들에 실린 작품들과 교차해서 확인한 후에 인용했다.

Thomas Hardy. *Selected Poetry*. Ed. Samuel Hynes. Oxford: Oxford UP, 1996.

W. B. Yeats. *The Collected Poems of W. B. Yeats*. Ed. Richard J. Finneran. New York: Collier Books, 1983.

W. H. Auden. *Collected Poems*. Ed. Edward Mendelson. New York: Vintage, 1976.

Dylan Thomas. *The Poems of Dylan Thomas*. Ed. Daniel Jones. New York: New Directions, 1971.

Philip Larkin. *Collected Poems*. Ed. Anthony Thwaite. New York: Farrar. Straus and Giroux, 1988.

Seamus Heaney. *Opened Ground: Selected Poems 1966-1996*. New York: Farrar. Straus and Giroux, 1998.

Carol Ann Duffy의 시 가운데 "Standing Female Nude"는 *Standing Female Nude*. London: Anvil, 1985에서, "Money Talks"와 "Warming Her Pearls"는 *Selling Manhattan*. London: Anvil, 1987에서, "Translating the English, 1989"는 *The Other Country*. London: Anvil, 1990에서, "Valentine"은 *Mean Time*. London: Anvil 1993에서, 그리고 "Anne Hathaway"는 *The World's Wife*. New York: Faber and Faber 1999에서 각각 가져왔다.

Edwin Arlington Robinson. *Tilbury Town: Selected Poems of Edwin Arlington Robinson*. Ed. Lawrance Thomson. New York: Macmillan, 1953.

Robert Frost. *The Poetry of Robert Frost*. Ed. Edward Connery Lathem. New York: Holt, Rinehart and Winston, 1969.

Wallace Stevens. *The Collected Poems of Wallace Stevens*. New York: Vintage 1982.

Langston Hughes. *The Collected Poems of Langston Hughes*. Ed. Arnold Rampersad. New York: Vintage, 1994.

Theodore Roethke. *The Collected Poems of Theodore Roethke*. New York: Anchor 1975.

Gary Snyder. *No Nature: New and Selected Poems*. New York: Pantheon Books, 1992.

Adrienne Rich, *The Fact of a Doorframe: Selected Poems 1950-2001*. New York: Norton, 2002.

2019년 8월

편저자 최동오

Contents

Wallace Stevens(1879-1955) / 172

Langston Hughes(1902-1967) / 190

Theodore Roethke(1908-1963) / 207

Gary Snyder(1930-) / 220

Adrienne Rich(1929-2012) / 236

현대 영미시의 이해

작가별로 읽기

Thomas Hardy(1840-1928)

Thomas Hardy, the son of a stonemason, was born in Dorset, England, on June 2, 1840. He trained as an architect and worked in London and Dorset for ten years. Hardy began his writing career as a novelist, publishing *Desperate Remedies* in 1871, and was soon successful enough to leave the field of architecture for writing. His novels *Tess of the D'Urbervilles* (1891) and *Jude the Obscure* (1895), which are considered literary classics today, received negative reviews upon publication and Hardy was criticized for being too pessimistic and preoccupied with sex. He left fiction writing for poetry, and published eight collections, including *Poems of the Past and the Present* (1902) and *Satires of Circumstance* (1914).

Hardy's poetry explores a fatalist outlook against the dark, rugged landscape of his native Dorset. He rejected the Victorian belief in a benevolent God, and much of his poetry reads as a sardonic lament on the bleakness of the human condition. A traditionalist in technique, he nevertheless forged a highly original style, combining rough-hewn rhythms and colloquial diction with an extraordinary variety of meters and stanzaic forms. A significant influence on later poets (including Frost, Auden, Dylan Thomas, and Philip Larkin), his influence has increased during the course of the century, offering an alternative — more down-to-earth, less rhetorical — to the more mystical and aristocratic precedent of Yeats. Thomas Hardy died on January 11, 1928.

Channel Firing

That night your great guns, unawares,
Shook all our coffins as we lay,
And broke the chancel window-squares,
We thought it was the Judgment-day

And sat upright. While drearisome
Arose the howl of wakened hounds:
The mouse let fall the altar-crumb,
The worms drew back into the mounds,

The glebe cow drooled. Till God called, "No;
It's gunnery practice out at sea
Just as before you went below;
The world is as it used to be:

"All nations striving strong to make
Red war yet redder. Mad as hatters
They do no more for Christés sake
Than you who are helpless in such matters.

"That this is not the judgment-hour
For some of them's a blessed thing,
For if it were they'd have to scour
Hell's floor for so much threatening....

"Ha, ha. It will be warmer when
I blow the trumpet (if indeed
I ever do; for you are men,
And rest eternal sorely need)."

해협 함포사격

당신의 대포들이, 무심코,
우리들이 누워 있는 관들을 온통 뒤흔들고
성단이 있는 쪽 창틀을 깨뜨렸던 그날밤
우리는 최후의 심판의 날이 왔다고 생각하여

똑바로 일어나 앉았었다. 한편 쓸쓸히
잠깬 사냥개들의 울부짖는 소리가 일어났다;
생쥐도 제단 빵부스러기를 떨어뜨리고
벌레들도 도로 무덤 속으로 물러났었다.

교회농장 소가 침을 질질 흘렸다. 하나님이 "아냐;
저건, 너희들이 지하로 내려가기 전과 꼭 같이
저 타다 밖에서 하는 함포사격이야,
세상은 늘 있었던 그대로야 :

"모든 국가들이 붉은 전쟁을 한층, 붉게
하려고 힘차게 애쓰고 있지. 아주 미쳐서
그들은 크리스트를 위해 아무 일도 하지 않아
그런 일에 무력한 너희들과 마찬가지로.

"지금이 최후의 심판의 시간이 아님은
몇몇 그들에겐 다행스런 일이지,
왜냐면 만일 그랬다면 그들은 많이 위협한 죄로
지옥의 바닥을 북북 문질러 닦아야만 할테니…

"하, 하. 내가 나팔을 부는 날이면
뜨거울거야 (정말이지 내가 그렇게
한다면 : 왜냐면 너희들은 인간이어서
휴식이 영원히 절실한 필요일 테니까)"

So down we lay again. "I wonder,
Will the world ever saner be,"
Said one, "than when He sent us under
In our indifferent century!"

And many a skeleton shook his head.
"Instead of preaching forty year,"
My neighbour Parson Thirdly said,
"I wish I had stuck to pipes and beer."

Again the guns disturbed the hour,
Roaring their readiness to avenge,
As far inland as Stourton Tower,
And Camelot, and starlit Stonehenge.

그래서 우리는 다시 누웠다. "도대체
세상이 언제 가서 더 정신을 차릴까"
하나가 말했다, "우리들의 무관심한 세기에
"하나님이 우리를 하계로 보낼 때보다!"

그리고 많은 해골들이 머리를 저었다.
"사십년을 설교하기보다."
내 이웃 써어들리 목사가 말했다,
"차라리 담배나 피우고 맥주나 마셨더라면 좋았을걸."

또다시 함포가 시간을 뒤흔들며
복수의 용의를 으르렁댔다,
스타우어튼 탑과 캐멜러트성,
그리고 별이 총총한 스토운헨지 내지로 멀리.

The Darkling Thrush

I leant upon a coppice gate
    When Frost was spectre-grey,
And Winter's dregs made desolate
    The weakening eye of day.
The tangled bine-stems scored the sky
    Like strings of broken lyres,
And all mankind that haunted nigh
    Had sought their household fires.

The land's sharp features seemed to be
    The Century's corpse outleant,
His crypt the cloudy canopy,
    The wind his death-lament.
The ancient pulse of germ and birth
    Was shrunken hard and dry,
And every spirit upon earth
    Seemed fervourless as I.

At once a voice arose among
    The bleak twigs overhead
In a full-hearted evensong
    Of joy illimited;
An aged thrush, frail, gaunt, and small,
    In blast-beruffled plume,
Had chosen thus to fling his soul
    Upon the growing gloom.

So little cause for carolings
    Of such ecstatic sound

어둠 속의 지빠귀 새

나는 잡목숲 문에 기대섰었다.
　　'서리'가 유령처럼 하얗고,
'겨울'의 눈꼽으로 희미한
　　태양의 눈이 침침해질 때.
뒤얽힌 담쟁이 덩굴이 부서진 칠현금의 현처럼
　　하늘에 금을 긋고
근처에 드나들던 사람들은 모두
　　집안의 불 가를 찾아들어 갔다.

대지의 형상들은 흡사
　　쓰러진 '세기'의 시체 같았다,
구름 덮인 하늘은 그 시신의 무덤이고
　　바람은 그 죽음의 장송곡.
배태와 출생의 오랜 맥박은
　　빳빳이 바싹 오그라들고,
지상의 일체의 생령은
　　나처럼 열정이 없어 보였다.

이 때 난데없이 한 목소리가 솟구쳐 나왔다,
　　머리 위의 삭막한 가지들 사이에서,
심혼을 기우려 불러대는
　　무한한 기쁨의 저녁기도가 되어.
연약하고, 야위고, 작고, 늙은 지빠귀새 한 마리,
　　강풍에 깃이 흐트러진 채
이렇게 저의 영혼을 쏟아내고자 했었다,
　　이 짙어지는 어둠에.

이토록 황홀하게 노래를 부를만한
　　원인이 보이지 않았다,

Was written on terrestrial things
    Afar or nigh around,
That I could think there trembled through
    His happy good-night air
Some blessed Hope, whereof he knew
    And I was unaware.

멀리 가까이 주변
　　지상의 사물들에.
그래서 나는 그 새의 행복한 저녁 인사의
　　노래 속에 어떤 축복의 '희망'이
고동치고 있건만 그것을 새만 알 뿐
　　나는 모르고 있다고 생각했다.

Hap

If but some vengeful god would call to me
From up the sky, and laugh: "Thou suffering thing,
Know that thy sorrow is my ecstasy,
That thy love's loss is my hate's profiting!"

Then would I bear it, clench myself, and die,
Steeled by the sense of ire unmerited:
Half-eased in that a Powerfuller than I
Had willed and meted me the tears I shed.

But not so. How arrives it joy lies slain,
And why unblooms the best hope ever sown?
—Crass Casualty obstructs the sun and rain,
And dicing Time for gladness casts a moan...
These purblind Doomsters had as readily strown
Blisses about my pilgrimage as pain

우연

어떤 복수심에 불타는 신이 하늘에서
나에게 "너 고통받는 자여, 너의 슬픔은
나의 큰 기쁨, 너의 사랑의 상실은
나의 미움의 이득임을 알지라"라고 외치면서 껄껄대고
　웃는다면

나는 그것을 꾹 참고서, 이를 악물고 죽을 것이다.
부당한 노여움을 샀구나 하는 생각에 몸이 굳어져,
나보다 '강력한 어떤 자'의 뜻으로 내가 흘리는 눈물이
나에게 벌로 주어졌구나 하고 반쯤 안심이 되어.

그러나 그렇지는 않다. 어떻게 오든 기쁨은 살해된다.
그리고 일찍이 씨 뿌려진 최선의 희망이 왜 꽃피지 못
　하고 시드는가.
— '우둔한 우연'이 해를 가리고 비를 막고,
주사위 던지는 '시간'이 기쁨 대신에 신음을 던지고…
이러한 반소경의 '운명의 사제들'이 나의 인생행로에
축복을 뿌리거나 고통을 뿌리거나 예사였기 때문이다.

In Time of "the Breaking of Nations"

I

Only a man harrowing clods
  In a slow silent walk
With an old horse that stumbles and nods
  Half asleep as they stalk.

II

Only thin smoke without flame
  From the heaps of couch-grass;
Yet this will go onward the same
  Though Dynasties pass.

III

Yonder a maid and her wight
  Come whispering by:
War's annals will cloud into night
  Ere their story die.

“나라들이 부서지는” 시기에

I

천천히 말없이 걸으며
  흙을 고르는 한 사람이 있을 뿐,
늙은 말 한 마리 데리고 비틀거리며 꾸벅거리며,
  사람이나 말이나 반쯤 졸면서 걷는다.

II

불길 없이 솟아오르는 연기 한 가닥,
  잡초 무더기에서.
그러나 이 상태는 지속되리라,
  왕조가 가고 또 가도.

III

저기에 처녀와 총각이
  속삭이며 온다.
전쟁의 역사는 어둠 속에 묻혀버리리라,
  저들의 얘기가 끝나기 전에.

Neutral Tones

We stood by a pond that winter day,
And the sun was white, as though chidden of God,
And a few leaves lay on the starving sod;
– They had fallen from an ash, and were gray.

Your eyes on me were as eyes that rove
Over tedious riddles of years ago;
And some words played between us to and fro
On which lost the more by our love.

The smile on your mouth was the deadest thing
Alive enough to have strength to die;
And a grin of bitterness swept thereby
Like an ominous bird a-wing⋯.

Since then, keen lessons that love deceives,
And wrings with wrong, have shaped to me
Your face, and the God curst sun, and a tree,
And a pond edged with grayish leaves.

잿빛 색조

그 겨울날 우리는 연못가에 서 있었다,
태양은 신에게 저주받은 듯이 하얗고,
생기 잃은 대지 위에 낙엽이 몇 개 떨어져 있었다.
— 물푸레나무에서 떨어져 색이 바랜.

나를 바라보는 당신의 눈은 오래전의
지루한 수수께끼를 더듬는 눈과 같았고,
우리 사이에 오고 간 몇 마디 말은
사랑의 빛이 바랜 말이었다.

너의 입가에 떠오른 미소는 그지없이 처량했다,
겨우 꺼져가는 힘밖에 없는.
그리하여 쓰디쓴 웃음이 스쳐갔다
마치 불길한 새가 날아가듯이…

그때 이래, 사랑은 속이는 것, 사랑은
악의로 괴롭히는 것이란 쓰라린 교훈과 더불어, 눈앞에
당신의 얼굴과 신에게 저주받은 태양과 한 그루 나무와
잿빛 낙엽에 에워싸인 연못이 윤곽을 드러낸다.

The Voice

Woman much missed, how you call to me, call to me,
Saying that now you are not as you were
When you had changed from the one who was all to me,
But as at first, when our day was fair.

Can it be you that I hear? Let me view you, then,
Standing as when I drew near to the town
Where you would wait for me: yes, as I knew you then,
Even to the original air-blue gown!

Or is it only the breeze, in its listlessness
Travelling across the wet mead to me here,
You being ever dissolved to wan wistlessness,
Heard no more again far or near?

Thus I; faltering forward,
Leaves around me falling,
Wind oozing thin through the thorn from norward,
And the woman calling.

목소리

사무치레 그리운 여인이여, 당신은 어떻게 내게 말을 하는 가요,
지금의 당신은 이전의 당신이 아니라고,
나에게 전부였던 그 당신이 변했던 시절, 그때가 아닌
우리 사이가 아름다웠던 처음 그때와 같다고 말하는군요.

들려오는 목소리가 정말로 당신인가요, 그렇다면 봅시다,
내가 집 근처 다가들면 늘 기다리고
서 있던 당신의 모습, 그래요, 그때 내가 보았던
그 상쾌한 하늘색 까운까지도 똑같은 당신의 모습을.

아니면, 이 목소리는 축축한 초원을 가로질러 무심히
이쪽으로 불어오는 미풍에 불과한가요,
당신의 목소리는 이제 파리한 불가해한 것으로 변하여
이 근처 어디서고 다시는 안 들리는군요.

  그래서 나는 비틀거리며 걸어가고,
  낙엽은 여기저기 떨어집니다.
바람은 북쪽에서 가시덤불 사이로 가냘프게 스며들고,
  여인의 부르는 목소리.

W. B. Yeats(1865-1939)

Born in Dublin, Ireland, on June 13, 1865, William Butler Yeats was the son of a well-known Irish painter, John Butler Yeats. He spent his childhood in County Sligo, where his parents were raised, and in London. He returned to Dublin at the age of fifteen to continue his education and study painting, but quickly discovered he preferred poetry. Born into the Anglo-Irish landowning class, Yeats became involved with the Celtic Revival, a movement against the cultural influences of English rule in Ireland during the Victorian period, which sought to promote the spirit of Ireland's native heritage. Though Yeats never learned Gaelic himself, his writing at the turn of the century drew extensively from sources in Irish mythology and folklore. Also a potent influence on his poetry was the Irish revolutionary Maud Gonne, whom he met in 1889, a woman equally famous for her passionate nationalist politics and her beauty. Though she married another man in 1903 and grew apart from Yeats (and Yeats himself was eventually married to another woman, Georgie Hyde Lees), she remained a powerful figure in his poetry.

Yeats was deeply involved in politics in Ireland, and in the twenties, despite Irish independence from England, his verse reflected a pessimism about the political situation in his country and the rest of Europe, paralleling the increasing conservativism of his American counterparts in London, T. S. Eliot and Ezra Pound. His work after 1910 was strongly influenced by Pound, becoming more modern in its concision and imagery, but Yeats never abandoned his strict adherence to traditional verse forms. He had a life-long interest in mysticism and the occult, which was off-putting to some readers, but he remained uninhibited in advancing his idiosyncratic philosophy, and his poetry continued to grow stronger as he grew older. Appointed a senator of the Irish Free State in 1922, he is remembered as an important cultural leader, as a major playwright (he was one of the founders of the famous Abbey Theatre in Dublin), and as one of the very greatest poets — in any language — of the century. W. B. Yeats was awarded the Nobel Prize in 1923 and died in 1939 at the age of seventy-three.

Among School children

I

I walk through the long schoolroom questioning;
A kind old nun in a white hood replies;
The children learn to cipher and to sing,
To study reading-books and history,
To cut and sew, be neat in everything
In the best modern way — the children's eyes
In momentary wonder stare upon
A sixty-year-old smiling public man.

II

I dream of a Ledaean body, bent
Above a sinking fire, a tale that she
Told of a harsh reproof, or trivial event
That changed some childish day to tragedy —
Told, and it seemed that our two natures blent
Into a sphere from youthful sympathy,
Or else, to alter Plato's parable,
Into the yolk and white of the one shell.

III

And thinking of that fit of grief or rage
I look upon one child or t'other there
And wonder if she stood so at that age —
For even daughters of the swan can share
Something of every paddler's heritage —

학교 어린이들 사이에서

I

나는 질문을 하면서 긴 교실을 걸어가고,
흰 후드를 쓴 한 친절한 노 수녀가 대답한다.
어린이들은 셈 공부, 노래 공부를 하고,
독본과 역사 공부도 하고,
재단과 재봉도 배우고, 여러 가지
최고의 현대적 기교를 배운다. — 아이들의 눈이
순간적으로 놀라서 일제히 쏠린다,
미소짓는 한 60세의 공인에게.

II

나는 레다와 같은 그녀의 모습을 그려본다,
그리고 꺼져가는 불 위에 허리를 구부리고 그녀가 얘기한
가혹한 책망이며, 어느 순진한 날을 비극으로 돌변시켰던
사소한 사건 같은 것을 상기한다 —
그것을 듣고서 우리 두 사람의 마음은
젊은 공감에서 한 구체로 융합되었었다,
달리 플라톤의 우화를 뒤집어 말한다면,
한 계란 속의 노른 자위와 흰 자위처럼 융합되었었다.

III

그 때 설움과 분노가 북받치던 것을 생각하면서
나는 여기에서 이 아이 저 아이를 쳐다본다.
그리고 그녀도 저 나이엔 저런 모습였을까 생각해본다 —
백조의 딸들이라 해도
뭇 물새의 유전이 깃들어 있는 것이니—

And had that colour upon cheek or hair,
And thereupon my heart is driven wild:
She stands before me as a living child.

IV

Her present image floats into the mind—
Did Quattrocento finger fashion it
Hollow of cheek as though it drank the wind
And took a mess of shadows for its meat?
And I though never of Ledaean kind
Had pretty plumage once—enough of that,
Better to smile on all that smile, and show
There is a comfortable kind of old scarecrow.

V

What youthful mother, a shape upon her lap
Honey of generation had betrayed,
And that must sleep, shriek, struggle to escape
As recollection or the drug decide,
Would think her son, did she but see that shape
With sixty or more winters on its head,
A compensation for the pang of his birth,
Or the uncertainty of his setting forth?

VI

Plato thought nature but a spume that plays
Upon a ghostly paradigm of things;
Solider Aristotle played the taws
Upon the bottom of a king of kings;

그리고 뺨과 머리 빛깔이 저러했을까 하고.
그런 생각을 하자 가슴이 설레고
그녀는 완연히 한 어린 아이로서 눈 앞에 서 있다.

IV

그녀의 현재의 영상이 마음 속에 어린다—
15세기 거장들의 손가락이 그런 모습을 만들었을까.
바람을 마시고, 고기 대신 그림자를
먹은 듯 두 뺨이 홀쭉하니.
그리고 나도 레다와 같은 족속은 아닐지라도
한때는 고운 깃이 있었다 — 그 정도로 그만 두자,
웃는 아이들에게 웃어 주고, 마음 편한
늙은 허수아비임을 보여주는 것이 좋을 듯.

V

생성의 꿀이 낳게 한 갓난 것,
그 약이 듣거나, 전생의 회상에 따라
잠들기도 하고, 소리 지르거나, 도망치려고 몸부림치는
어린 것을 무릎에 올려 놓은 젊은 어머니로서,
그것이 머리 위에 60년의 세월을 얹고 있는 것을
보았다면 대체 그것을
산고의 보상으로
또는 그것을 낳을 때의 불안의 값으로 생각하겠는가.

VI

플라톤은 자연을 그림자 같은 만물의 원형 위에
어릿거리는 물거품으로 생각했고,
한층 견실한 아리스토텔레스는 왕중 왕의
엉덩이에 매질을 가했었다.

World-famous golden-thighed Pythagoras
Fingered upon a fiddle-stick or strings
What a star sang and careless Muses heard:
Old clothes upon old sticks to scare a bird.

VII

Both nuns and mothers worship images,
But those the candles light are not as those
That animate a mother's reveries,
But keep a marble or a bronze repose.
And yet they too break hearts — O Presences
That passion, piety or affection knows,
And that all heavenly glory symbolise —
O self-born mockers of man's enterprise;

VIII

Labour is blossoming or dancing where
The body is not bruised to pleasure soul,
Nor beauty born out of its own despair,
Nor blear-eyed wisdom out of midnight oil.
O chestnut tree, great rooted blossomer,
Are you the leaf, the blossom or the bole?
O body swayed to music, O brightening glance,
How can we know the dancer from the dance?

세상에서 유명한 황금 넓적다리의 피타고라스는
바이올린의 활과 현에 손을 대어
별이 노래 부르면 무심한 시신이 귀 기울이던 곡을 켰다.
그러나 낡은 막대기에 낡은 옷가지 걸치고 새 쫓는 이 꼴.

VII

수녀들이나 어머니들은 이미지를 숭배한다.
그러나 촛불이 밝히는 이미지들은 어머니의 환상을
생기 있게 하는 그것과 같진 않고,
대리석이나 청동의 안정을 간직한다.
그렇지만 그것도 역시 가슴을 아프게 한다 — 아, '실재'여.
정렬과 경건과 애정이 알고 있는 그것,
그리고 온갖 천국의 영광이 상징하는 그것 —
아, 스스로 제 몸에서 생겨 인간의 일을 조롱하는 자여.

VIII

활동이 꽃피고 춤추는 그 곳에선
영을 즐겁게 하기 위하여 육체가 상처 입지 않고,
미는 자체의 실망에서 나오는 것이 아니고,
흐린 눈의 지혜는 철야 공부에서 나오지 않는다.
아, 밤나무야, 크게 뿌리 박고 꽃피는 자여,
너는 대체 잎이냐, 꽃이냐, 아니면 줄기냐?
아, 음악에 따라 흔들리는 육체여, 아, 빛나는 눈짓이여,
우리가 어떻게 댄서와 댄스를 구별하겠는가.

The Lake Isle of Innisfree

I will arise and go now, and go to Innisfree,
And a small cabin build there, of clay and wattles made;
Nine bean-rows will I have there, a hive for the honey-bee,
And live alone in the bee-loud glade.

And I shall have some peace there, for peace comes dropping slow,
Dropping from the veils of the morning to where the cricket sings;
There midnight's all a glimmer, and noon a purple glow,
And evening full of the linnet's wings.

I will arise and go now, for always night and day
I hear lake water lapping with low sounds by the shore;
While I stand on the roadway, or on the pavements grey,
I hear it in the deep heart's core.

호수의 섬 이니스프리

이제 나는 일어나 가야겠다. 이니스프리로 가야겠다,
거기에 진흙과 외를 엮어 작은 오두막집 한 칸 짓고,
또한 거기에 아홉 이랑의 콩밭과 꿀벌 한 통 가지련다.
그리고서 벌 소리 요란한 골짜기에 홀로 살련다.

그러면 거기 평화가 있겠지, 평화는 천천히 방울져 내리겠지,
아침 장막으로부터 귀뚜라미 우는 곳에까지.
그곳, 한밤은 온통 희미하게 빛나고, 대낮은 보랏빛 광채,
그리고 저녁은 홍방울새 날개로 가득히 차.

이제 나는 일어나 가야겠다, 밤이나 낮이나 항상
호수 물이 낮게 기슭에 찰싹이는 소리 들리니.
가로에 섰을 때나 회색 포도 위에 섰을 때나
내겐 그 소리가 깊이 가슴 한복판에 들린다.

Leda and the Swan

A sudden blow: the great wings beating still
Above the staggering girl, her thighs caressed
By the dark webs, her nape caught in his bill,
He holds her helpless breast upon his breast.

How can those terrified vague fingers push
The feathered glory from her loosening thighs?
And how can body, laid in that white rush,
But feel the strange heart beating where it lies?

A shudder in the loins engenders there
The broken wall, the burning roof and tower
And Agamemnon dead.
                    Being so caught up,
So mastered by the brute blood of the air,
Did she put on his knowledge with his power
Before the indifferent beak could let her drop?

레다와 백조

급습. 백조는 큰 두 날개를
비틀거리는 여인 위에서 조용히 친다. 여인의 허벅다리는
새의 검은 두 지막에 쓰다듬기고, 목은 부리에 잡혀,
어찌 할 수 없이 여인의 가슴은 백조의 가슴에 껴안긴다.

겁에 질려 힘 빠진 손가락이 어떻게 맥풀린 허벅다리에서
깃에 싸인 그 영광을 밀어 젖힐 수 있겠는가.
백색의 급습에 내맡긴 육체가 그 품 안에서
이상히 가슴 울렁임을 느끼지 않을 수 있으랴.

허리에 느꼈던 그 떨림에서
무너진 벽과 불타는 지붕과 탑과
아가멤논의 죽음이 생겨난 것이다.
하늘에서 온 그 짐승 같은 피에
그토록 붙잡혀 정복 당하였으니,
언제 보았냐는 듯이 그 주둥이가 여인을 놓기 전에
그녀는 과연 그의 예지와 힘을 함께 전해 받은 것일까.

Sailing to Byzantium

I

That is no country for old men. The young
In one another's arms, birds in the trees,
—Those dying generations—at their song,
The salmon-falls, the mackerel-crowded seas,
Fish, flesh, or fowl, commend all summer long
Whatever is begotten, born, and dies.
Caught in that sensual music all neglect
Monuments of unageing intellect.

II

An aged man is but a paltry thing,
A tattered coat upon a stick, unless
Soul clap its hands and sing, and louder sing
For every tatter in its mortal dress,
Nor is there singing school but studying
Monuments of its own magnificence;
And therefore I have sailed the seas and come
To the holy city of Byzantium.

III

O sages standing in God's holy fire
As in the gold mosaic of a wall,
Come from the holy fire, perne in a gyre,
And be the singing-masters of my soul.
Consume my heart away; sick with desire

비잔티움으로의 항해

I

저것은 늙은 사람들의 나라가 아니다.
팔에 팔을 낀 젊은이들, 숲속의 새들,
— 저 죽음의 생명체들은 — 저희들의 노래에 취하고,
연어 오르는 폭포, 고등어 우글거리는 바다
고기나 짐승이나 새들은 온 여름 동안
생겨서 나서 죽는 온갖 것들을 찬양한다.
모두들 관능의 음악에 취하여
늙지 않는 이지의 기념비적 의미를 모르는구나.

II

늙은 사람이란 정말 보잘 것 없는 것,
막대기에 걸친 누더기 등거리이다,
육체의 옷이 갈기갈기 찢어지는 것을 영혼이
손뼉치며 노래하지 않고, 소리 높여 노래하지 않는다면,
또한 영혼의 장엄한 기념비적 의미를 배우지 않는다면,
노래를 배울 곳은 아무데도 없다.
그래서 나는 바다를 건너
이 곳 성시 비잔티움에 왔다.

III

아! 벽에 아로새긴 황금 모자이크 사이에 있듯이
신의 성스런 불 속에 서 있는 성자들이여,
그 성화로부터 나와, 하나의 원을 그리며 선회하사
내 영혼에 노래를 가르치는 스승이 되시라.
그리고 내 심장을 소멸시키시라, 욕정에 병들고

And fastened to a dying animal
It knows not what it is; and gather me
Into the artifice of eternity.

IV

Once out of nature I shall never take
My bodily form from any natural thing,
But such a form as Grecian goldsmiths make
Of hammered gold and gold enamelling
To keep a drowsy Emperor awake;
Or set upon a golden bough to sing
To lords and ladies of Byzantium
Of what is past, or passing, or to come.

죽음의 동물성에 얽매여
스스로를 깨닫지 못하는 그 심장을.
그리하여 나를 끌어들이시라 영원한 예술 안으로.

IV

한 번 자연에서 벗어난 후엔 다시는
내 형체를 어떤 자연물에서도 취하지 않고,
그리스의 금 세공인들이 메질한 금덩이와
황금 유약으로 만든 그런 형체를 취하련다,
황제의 졸음을 깨우기 위하여,
또는 황금 가지 위에 앉혀 비잔티움의 귀족 남녀들에게
과거와 현재와 미래를
노래해 들려주기 위하여 쓰였던.

When You Are Old

When you are old and grey and full of sleep,
And nodding by the fire, take down this book,
And slowly read, and dream of the soft look
Your eyes had once, and of their shadows deep;

How many loved your moments of glad grace,
And loved your beauty with love false or true,
But one man loved the pilgrim soul in you,
And loved the sorrows of your changing face;

And bending down beside the glowing bars,
Murmur, a little sadly, how Love fled
And paced upon the mountains overhead
And hid his face amid a crowd of stars.

그대 늙었을 때

그대 늙어 백발이 되어 졸음이 자꾸 오고
벽로 가에서 고개를 끄떡끄떡할 때, 이 책을 꺼내어,
천천히 읽으며 그대 눈이 옛날 지녔던
부드러운 눈동자와 그 깊은 그림자를 꿈꾸어라;

얼마나 많은 사람이 그대의 즐거운 우아의 순간을 사랑했으며,
또 그대의 미를 참사랑 혹은 거짓사랑으로 사랑했던가를,
그러나 오직 한 사람 그대의 편력하는 영혼을 사랑했고,
그대의 변해가는 얼굴의 슬픔을 사랑했었음을;

그리고 달아오르는 쇠살대 곁에 몸을 구부리고서,
좀 슬프게 중얼대어라, 어떻게 사랑이
산 위로 하늘 높이 도망치듯 달아나
그의 얼굴을 무수한 별들 사이에 감추었는가를.

The Wild Swans at Coole

The trees are in their autumn beauty,
The woodland paths are dry,
Under the October twilight the water
Mirrors a still sky;
Upon the brimming water among the stones
Are nine-and-fifty swans.

The nineteenth autumn has come upon me
Since I first made my count;
I saw, before I had well finished,
All suddenly mount
And scatter wheeling in great broken rings
Upon their clamorous wings.

I have looked upon those brilliant creatures,
And now my heart is sore.
All's changed since I, hearing at twilight,
The first time on this shore,
The bell-beat of their wings above my head,
Trod with a lighter tread.

Unwearied still, lover by lover,
They paddle in the cold
Companionable streams or climb the air;
Their hearts have not grown old;
Passion or conquest, wander where they will,
Attend upon them still.

쿨호의 야생 백조

나무들은 제각기 곱게 가을로 단장하고,
숲속 길들은 메마르다.
10월달 석양 아래 물은
고요한 하늘을 비추며,
돌과 돌 사이 넘치는 물 위엔
백조가 쉰 아홉 마리.

처음에 저 수효를 세어 본 이래
열 아홉 번째 가을이 닥쳐 왔구나.
채 다 세기도 전에
후르릉 모두 날아 올라
날개 소리도 요란하게
단절된 큰 원을 그리며 선회하다 흩어지곤 하더니.

저 눈부신 새들을 보고 있노라니,
이제 가슴이 아프다.
모든 것이 변했구나, 해질 무렵,
이 호수가에서 처음으로
머리 위에 쇳소리 같은 날개 소리 들었을 때는
발걸음도 가볍게 거닐었는데.

여전히 피곤을 모르고, 사랑하는 것들 끼리끼리
차디찬 다정한 물 속에 헤엄치거나,
중천에 솟아오르는구나.
그들의 가슴은 늙지 않아,
열정과 패기가 가는 곳 어디서나,
항상 그들을 따르는구나,

But now they drift on the still water,
Mysterious, beautiful;
Among what rushes will they build,
By what lake's edge or pool
Delight men's eyes when I awake some day
To find they have flown away?

이제 저것들 고요한 물 위에
신비롭과 아름답게 떠 있다.
내 언젠가 잠 깨어 저것들 날아가 없음을 알게되는 그날엔
저것들 어느 호수 가에, 어느 웅덩이 가에,
어떤 골풀 사이에 집 짓고
사람들의 눈을 즐겁게 할 것인가.

W. H. Auden (1907-1973)

Wystan Hugh Auden was born in York, England, on February 21, 1907. He moved to Birmingham during childhood and was educated at Christ Church, Oxford. As a young man he was influenced by the poetry of Thomas Hardy and Robert Frost, as well as William Blake, Emily Dickinson, Gerard Manley Hopkins, and Old English verse. At Oxford his precocity as a poet was immediately apparent, and he formed lifelong friendships with two fellow writers, Stephen Spender and Christopher Isherwood.

In 1928, his collection *Poems* was privately printed, but it wasn't until 1930, when another collection titled *Poems* (though its contents were different) was published, that Auden was established as the leading voice of a new generation.

Ever since, he has been admired for his unsurpassed technical virtuosity and an ability to write poems in nearly every imaginable verse form; the incorporation in his work of popular culture, current events, and vernacular speech; and also for the vast range of his intellect, which drew easily from an extraordinary variety of literatures, art forms, social and political theories, and scientific and technical information. He had a remarkable wit, and often mimicked the writing styles of other poets such as Dickinson, W. B. Yeats, and Henry James. His poetry frequently recounts, literally or metaphorically, a journey or quest, and his travels provided rich material for his verse.

He visited Germany, Iceland, and China, served in the

Spanish Civil war, and in 1939 moved to the United States, where he met his lover, Chester Kallman, and became an American citizen. His own beliefs changed radically between his youthful career in England, when he was an ardent advocate of socialism and Freudian psychoanalysis, and his later phase in America, when his central preoccupation became Christianity and the theology of modern Protestant theologians. A prolific writer, Auden was also a noted playwright, librettist, editor, and essayist. Generally considered the greatest English poet of the twentieth century, his work has exerted a major influence on succeeding generations of poets on both sides of the Atlantic.

W. H. Auden served as a chancellor of the Academy of American Poets from 1954 to 1973, and divided most of the second half of his life between residences in New York City and Austria. He died in Vienna on September 29, 1973.

Funeral Blues

Stop all the clocks, cut off the telephone,
Prevent the dog from barking with a juicy bone,
Silence the pianos and with muffled drum
Bring out the coffin, let the mourners come.

Let aeroplanes circle moaning overhead
Scribbling on the sky the message He Is Dead,
Put crepe bows round the white necks of the public doves,
Let the traffic policemen wear black cotton gloves.

He was my North, my South, my East and West,
My working week and my Sunday rest,
My noon, my midnight, my talk, my song;
I thought that love would last for ever: I was wrong.

The stars are not wanted now: put out every one;
Pack up the moon and dismantle the sun;
Pour away the ocean and sweep up the wood.
For nothing now can ever come to any good.

장례식 블루스

모든 시계를 멈춰라, 전화를 끊어라.
기름진 뼈다귀를 물려 개가 못 짖게 하라.
피아노들을 침묵하게 하고 천을 두른 북을 쳐
관이 들어오게 하라. 조문객들을 들여보내라.

비행기를 하늘에 띄워 신음하며 돌게 하고,
그가 죽었다는 메시지를 하늘에 휘갈기게 하라.
거리의 비둘기들 하얀 목에 검은 상장을 두르고,
교통경찰에게는 검은 면장갑을 끼게 하라.

그는 나의 동쪽이고 서쪽이며 남쪽이고 북쪽이었다.
나의 평일의 생활이자 일요일의 휴식이었고,
나의 정오, 나의 자정, 나의 대화, 나의 노래였다.
우리 사랑이 영원할 줄 알았으나, 내가 틀렸다.

별들은 이제 필요 없다, 모두 다 꺼버려라,
달을 싸버리고 해를 철거해라,
바다를 쏟아버리고 숲을 쓸어버려라,
이제는 그 무엇도 아무 소용이 없으리니.

Ganymede

He looked in all His wisdom from the throne
Down on that humble boy who kept the sheep,
And sent a dove; the dove returned alone:
Youth liked the music, but soon fell asleep.

But He had planned such future for the youth:
Surely, His duty now was to compel.
For later he would come to love the truth,
And own his gratitude. His eagle fell.

It did not work. His conversation bored
The boy who yawned and whistled and made faces,
And wriggled free from fatherly embraces;

But with the eagle he was always willing
To go where it suggested, and adored
And learnt from it so many ways of killing.

가누메데스

그는 옥좌에서 그의 모든 지혜를 모아
양을 돌보던 그 미천한 소년을 내려다보았고,
비둘기를 보냈으나 그 비둘기는 홀로 돌아왔다.
젊은이는 음악을 좋아했고 곧 잠에 빠졌다.

그는 젊은이를 위해 미래의 계획을 세웠다.
분명, 강요하는 게 그의 본분이었다.
나중에 그는 진실을 좋아하게 될 것이고
감사를 표하게 될 것이기에. 그의 독수리가 낙하했다.

효과가 없었다. 그의 대화는 지루해서
소년은 하품을 했으며 휘슬을 불며 얼굴을 찌푸렸고
자애로운 포옹에서 벗어나려 꿈틀거렸다.

하지만 그는 독수리가 제시하는 곳으로 기꺼이
함께 갈 채비가 되어 있었고 독수리에게서
수많은 죽임의 방법을 배웠고 숭배했다.

Lullaby

Lay your sleeping head, my love,
Human on my faithless arm;
Time and fevers burn away
Individual beauty from
Thoughtful children, and the grave
Proves the child ephemeral:
But in my arms till break of day
Let the living creature lie,
Mortal, guilty, but to me
The entirely beautiful.

Soul and body have no bounds:
To lovers as they lie upon
Her tolerant enchanted slope
In their ordinary swoon,
Grave the vision Venus sends
Of supernatural sympathy,
Universal love and hope;
While an abstract insight wakes
Among the glaciers and the rocks
The hermit's carnal ecstasy.

Certainty, fidelity
On the stroke of midnight pass
Like vibrations of a bell,
And fashionable madmen raise
Their pedantic boring cry:
Every farthing of the cost,
All the dreaded cards foretell,

자장가

애인이여, 잠든 머리를 눕혀라,
인간의 몸을 믿음성 없는 나의 이 팔에.
시간과 광열이
철이 든 아이들로부터
하나하나 그 개개의 미를 태워버리고, 무덤은
그 아이의 덧없음을 입증한다.
그러나 내 두 팔 안에 날이 샐 때까지
살아 있는 그 몸을 누워 있게 하라,
죽음을 면치 못하고 죄에 가득찬 것이지만
내게는 다시없이 아름다운 그것을.

영혼과 육체는 구분이 없다.
언제나 다름없이 황홀 지경에서
여자의 넉넉한 매혹적인 경사 위에
몸을 눕히는 애인들에게,
사랑의 여신 비너스는 엄숙히 보낸다
신비 스런 조화의 환상과
보편적 사랑과 희망을.
한편 추상적 통찰력은
빙하와 바위산 사이에서
은자의 황홀한 육욕을 눈뜨게 한다.

확신이나 충성심은
한 밤중 시계 소리에
종의 진동처럼 사라지고,
시류를 쫓는 미치광이들은 웨친다,
아는 체하고 싫증나는 부르짖음을.
모든 무서운 카드들은 예언하기를
한푼의 비용도 모조리

Shall be paid, but from this night
Not a whisper, not a thought,
Not a kiss nor look be lost.

Beauty, midnight, vision dies:
Let the winds of dawn that blow
Softly round your dreaming head
Such a day of welcome show
Eye and knocking heart may bless,
Find the mortal world enough;
Noons of dryness find you fed
By the involuntary powers,
Nights of insult let you pass
Watched by every human love.

갚아야 한다고. 그러나 오늘 밤 이후는
한 마디 속삭임도 한 가닥의 생각도
한번의 키쓰도 하나의 시선도 헛될 수는 없다.

아름다움도 한밤중도 비전도 사라진다.
꿈꾸는 그대 머리맡을 부드럽게 부는
새벽 바람으로 하여금
이토록 반가운 날을 있게 하라,
눈과 고동치는 가슴이 기쁨에 넘치고,
덧 없는 세상이나마 만족할 수 있게.
해가 비치는 대낮에는 그대에게
자기도 모르는 힘이 부여되고,
모멸의 밤에는
인간의 사랑의 수호 아래 보낼 수 있게.

Musee des Beaux Arts

About suffering they were never wrong,
The Old Masters: how well they understood
Its human position; how it takes place
While someone else is eating or opening a window or just walking dully along;
How, when the aged are reverently, passionately waiting
For the miraculous birth, there always must be
Children who did not specially want it to happen, skating
On a pond at the edge of the wood:
They never forgot
That even the dreadful martyrdom must run its course
Anyhow in a corner, some untidy spot
Where the dogs go on with their doggy life and the torturer's horse
Scratches its innocent behind on a tree.

In Brueghel's Icarus for instance: how everything turns away
Quite leisurely from the disaster; the ploughman may
Have heard the splash, the forsaken cry,
But for him it was not an important failure; the sun shone
As it had to on the white legs disappearing into the green
Water; and the expensive delicate ship that must have seen
Something amazing, a boy falling out of the sky,
Had somewhere to get to and sailed calmly on.

미술관

고난에 대해서 그들은 옳게 생각했다,
'옛 거장들.' 그들은 참 잘 이해했다,
인간에게 있어서의 고난의 위치를, 그것이 어떻게 일어
  나는가를,
누군가가 식사를 하거나, 창문을 열거나 또는 멍청하게
  길을 걸을 때에.
노인들이 경건하게, 열정적으로 기적적인 탄생을
기다릴 때에, 한편에선 그것이 일어나기를
별로 기다리지 않고 숲가의 연못에서
스케이트를 타는 아이들이 반드시 있다는 것을.
그들은 결코 잊지 않았다,
무서운 순교 조차 어느 구석에서
진행되고 있고, 어느 지저분한 구석에선
개들이 개의 생활을 하고 있고, 박해자의 말이
죄없는 엉덩이를 나무에 긁어댄다.

예컨대 브뤼겔의 그림 「이카루스」가 그렇다. 모든 것이
아주 유연하게 그 재난에서 고개를 돌린다. 농부는
어쩌면 물 튀기는 소리를, 절망의 외침을 들었을 것인데
그 농부에게 그런 것은 중대한 실패가 아니었다. 태양이
전에도 비쳤듯이 그 흰 두 발이 푸른 물 속으로 사라지는 것을
비치고 있었고, 저 우아한 호화선은 무엇인가 놀라운 것,
한 소년이 하늘에서 떨어지는 것을 보았음에 틀림 없는 데,
어딘가 갈 곳을 정하고 태연히 항해하고 있었다.

Petition

Sir, no man's enemy, forgiving all
But will his negative inversion, be prodigal:
Send to us power and light, a sovereign touch
Curing the intolerable neural itch,
The exhaustion of weaning, the liar's quinsy,
And the distortions of ingrown virginity.
Prohibit sharply the rehearsed response
And gradually correct the coward's stance;
Cover in time with beams those in retreat
That, spooted, they turn though the reverse were great;
Publish each healer that in city lives
Or country houses at the end of drives;
Harrow the house of the dead; look shining at
New styles of architecture, a change of heart.

청원

임이여, 아무의 적도 아니신, 의지라는 그 부정적 도착 이외는
모든 것을 용서하시는 임이여, 아낌없이 주시라.
힘과 빛을 우리에게, 그리고 지고한 손으로 어루만지셔
견딜 수 없는 신경의 가려움과,
젖 떨어질 때의 쇠약과 거짓말쟁이의 편두선염과
안에서 생기는 처녀의 왜곡증을 치료하시라,
되풀이하는 응답을 준엄하게 못하게 하시고
엉거주춤한 비겁한 자는 서서히 고치시라.
꽁무늬 빼는 자에겐 적당한 때에 광선을 퍼부으셔
발각되어 되돌아서게 하시라, 그 역전이 힘들겠지만.
도시에 사는 신앙 요법사를 하나하나 폭로하고
도로 끝에 있는 향사의 저택을 내보이시라.
사자의 집을 파헤치시라. 그리고 빛나는 눈으로
새 스타일의 건물과 새로워진 심장을 보시라.

The unknown citizen

(*To JS/07/M/378 This Marble Monument Is Erected by the State*)

He was found by the Bureau of Statistics to be
One against whom there was no official complaint,
And all the reports of his conduct agree
That, in the modern sense of the old-fashioned word, he was a saint,
For in everything he did he served the Greater Community.
Except for the war till the day he retired
He worked in a factory and never got fired,
But satisfied his employers, Fudge Motors Inc.
Yet he wasn't a scab or odd in his views,
For his union reports that he paid his dues,
(Our report of his union shows it was sound)
And our Social Psychology workers found
That he was popular with his mates and liked a drink.
The Press are convinced that he bought a paper every day,
And that his reactions to advertisements were normal in every way.
Policies taken out in his name prove that he was fully insured,
And his Health-card shows that he was once in hospital but
left it cured.
Both Producers Research and High—Grade Living declare
He was fully sensible to the advantages of the Installment Plan
And had everything necessary to the Modern Man,
A gramophone, a radio, a car and a frigidaire.
Our researchers into Public Opinion are content
That he held the proper opinions for the time of the year;
When there was peace he was for peace; when there was war he went.

무명 시민

(JS/07/M/378에게 이 대리석 기념비는 국가가 건립한 것이다)

그는 통계국에 의해 판명되었다
당국에 대해 불평이 전혀 없는 사람이라고
그리고 그의 행위에 관한 모든 보고는 일치한다
낡은 단어의 현대식 의미에서 그는 성인이었다고
왜냐하면 그가 한 모든 일에서 그는 큰 공동사회에 봉사했으니까.
전쟁 때를 빼놓고 은퇴하는 날까지
공장에서 일했으며, 한 번도 해고당한 적 없이
퍼지 자동차회사의 고용주들을 만족시켰다.
그는 비조합원도 아니었고 이상한 견해도 갖지 않았다
왜냐하면 그의 조합은 그가 회비를 내었다고 보고했고,
(그의 조합에 관한 우리 보고서가 그것이 올바름을 보여 준다)
그리고 우리 사회심리학 연구자들은
그가 동료 간에 인기가 있고 술을 좋아했음을 발견했다.
신문사는 그가 매일 신문을 샀고
광고에 대한 그의 반응이 모든 면에서 정상적이었음을 확신한다.
그의 명의로 든 보험증권은 그가 피보험자임을 입증해주고
그의 보험증은 그가 한번 입원한 일이 있으나 치료받고 퇴원했음을 보여준다.
생산성 연구와 고급 생활은 확언한다
그가 월부의 편리에 아주 민감하고
현대인에 필요한 전부를
축음기, 라디오, 자동차, 냉장고를 갖고 있다고.
우리 여론조사들은 흡족해 한다
그가 시사에 관해 올바른 의견을 가졌음을
평화 시에 그는 평화를 지지했고 전시에는 출전했다.

He was married and added five children to the population,
which our Eugenist says was the right number for a parent of
his generation,
And our teachers report he never interfered with their education.
Was he free? Was he happy? The question is absurd:
Had anything been wrong, we should certainly have heard.

그는 결혼하여 인구에 다섯 애들을 추가했고
우리 우생학자들은 그것이 그의 세대 같은 아버지에겐 알맞은
숫자였다고 말한다.
그리고 우리 선생님들은 그가 그들의 교육에 한 번도 간섭하지
않았다고 보고한다.
그는 자유로웠던가? 그는 행복했던가? 그런 질문은 당치도 않다.
뭔가 잘못된 데가 있었더라면, 우리는 어김없이 보고받았을테니까.

Dylan Thomas (1914-1953)

Dylan Marlais Thomas was born on October 27, 1914, in Swansea, South Wales. His father was an English Literature professor at the local grammar school and would often recite Shakespeare to Thomas before he could read. He loved the sounds of nursery rhymes, foreshadowing his love for the rhythmic ballads of Gerard Manley Hopkins, W. B. Yeats, and Edgar Allan Poe. Although both of his parents spoke fluent Welsh, Thomas and his older sister never learned the language, and Thomas wrote exclusively in English.

Unlike his contemporaries, T. S. Eliot and W. H. Auden, Thomas was not concerned with exhibiting themes of social and intellectual issues, and his writing, with its intense lyricism and highly charged emotion, has more in common with the Romantic tradition.

Thomas describes his technique in a letter: "I make one image—though 'make' is not the right word; I let, perhaps, an image be 'made' emotionally in me and then apply to it what intellectual & critical forces I possess—let it breed another, let that image contradict the first, make, of the third image bred out of the other two together, a fourth contradictory image, and let them all, within my imposed formal limits, conflict."

About Thomas's work, Michael Schmidt writes: "There is a kind of authority to the word magic of the early poems; in the famous and popular later poems, the magic is all show. If they have a secret it is the one we all share, partly erotic, partly elegiac. The later poems arise out of personality."

In 1940, Thomas and his wife moved to London. He had served as an anti-aircraft gunner but was rejected for more active combat due to illness. To avoid the air raids, the couple left London in 1944. They eventually settled at Laugharne, in the Boat House where Thomas would write many of his later poems.

Thomas toured America four times, with his last public engagement taking place at the City College of New York. A few days later, he collapsed in the Chelsea Hotel after a long drinking bout at the White Horse Tavern. On November 9, 1953, he died at St. Vincent's Hospital in New York City at the age of thirty-nine. He had become a legendary figure, both for his work and the boisterousness of his life. He was buried in Laugharne, and almost thirty years later, a plaque to Dylan was unveiled in Poet's Corner, Westminster Abbey.

And Death Shall Have No Dominion

And death shall have no dominion.
Dead man naked they shall be one
With the man in the wind and the west moon;
When their bones are picked clean and the clean bones gone,
They shall have stars at elbow and foot;
Though they go mad they shall be sane,
Though they sink through the sea they shall rise again;
Though lovers be lost love shall not;
And death shall have no dominion.

And death shall have no dominion.
Under the windings of the sea
They lying long shall not die windily;
Twisting on racks when sinews give way,
Strapped to a wheel, yet they shall not break;
Faith in their hands shall snap in two,
And the unicorn evils run them through;
Split all ends up they shan't crack;
And death shall have no dominion.

And death shall have no dominion.
No more may gulls cry at their ears
Or waves break loud on the seashores;
Where blew a flower may a flower no more
Lift its head to the blows of the rain;
Though they be mad and dead as nails,
Heads of the characters hammer through daisies;
Break in the sun till the sun breaks down,
And death shall have no dominion.

그리고 죽음이 권세 부르지 못하리라

그리고 죽음이 권세 부리지 못하리라.
알몸의 죽은 자들,
바람과 서녘달 사람과 하나 될 것이며,
저들 뼈가 깨끗이 씻기고 깨끗한 뼈마저 사라진 다음,
팔꿈치와 발꿈치에 별들을 가지리라.
미칠지라도 온전할 것이며
바다 속에 가라앉을지라도 다시 솟으리라.
애인들은 잃으나 사랑은 안 잃을 것이라.
그리고 죽음이 권세 부리지 못하리라.

그리고 죽음이 권세 부리지 못하리라.
바다의 수의에 감겨 오래 누운 자들
바람처럼 죽지 않으리라.
물레바퀴 고문대에 매여 힘줄 비틀려 끊겨도,
저들은 끊기지 않으리라.
손 안에 든 신앙은 두 조각나고,
일각수 괴물 같은 악이 저들을 꿰뚫고,
마디마디 모두 부셔져도, 저들은 깨지지 않으리라.
그리고 죽음이 권세 부리지 못하리라.

그리고 죽음이 권세 부리지 못하리라.
갈매기들 저들의 귀에 소리치지 못하고,
파도들 바닷가에 큰소리로 부딪치지 못하나,
꽃 피어나던 곳에 비의 감촉이 있어도,
꽃이 그 머리를 쳐들지 못하나,
저들이 미치고 쇠못처럼 죽었어도,
글자의 머리들이 들국화 줄기 통해 두들겨 나올 것이며
해가 소멸할 때까지 햇빛 속에 터져 나오리라.
그리고 죽음이 권세 부리지 못하리라.

Do Not Go Gentle into That Good Night

Do not go gentle into that good night,
Old age should burn and rave at close of day;
Rage, rage against the dying of the light.

Though wise men at their end know dark is right,
Because their words had forked no lightning they
Do not go gentle into that good night.

Good men, the last wave by, crying how bright
Their frail deeds might have danced in a green bay,
Rage, rage against the dying of the light.

Wild men who caught and sang the sun in flight,
And learn, too late, they grieved it on its way,
Do not go gentle into that good night.

Grave men, near death, who see with blinding sight
Blind eyes could blaze like meteors and be gay,
Rage, rage against the dying of the light.

And you, my father, there on that sad height,
Curse, bless, me now with your fierce tears, I pray.
Do not go gentle into that good night.
Rage, rage against the dying of the light.

저 좋은 밤으로 얌전히 들어가지 마소서

저 좋은 밤으로 얌전히 들어가지 마소서,
노년은 날 저물 때 미친 듯 분내고 외쳐야 합니다,
빛이 꺼져감에 격노해요, 격노하소서.

현자들은 최후를 맞을 때 어둠이 마땅함을 알지만,
그들의 말이 번개를 치게 한 적 없기에 그들은
저 좋은 밤으로 얌전히 들어가지 않습니다.

착한 사람들은, 마지막 물결이 지나간 뒤, 얼마나 밝게
그들의 연약한 행위들이 초록 포구에서 춤추었을지 외치면서
빛이 꺼져감에 격노합니다, 격노합니다.

날아가는 태양을 붙잡아 노래한 뒤,
제 갈길 가는 태양을 비통해 함을 너무 늦게 배운 방종한 자들은
저 좋은 밤으로 얌전히 들어가지 않습니다.

앞못보는 눈도 유성처럼 타오르고 유쾌해질 수 있음을
감겨져 가는 눈으로 보는, 죽음이 임박한 진지한 사람들은
빛이 꺼져감에 격노합니다, 격노합니다.

그러니 아버지, 나의 아버지여, 거기 슬픈 고지에서
이제 당신의 격렬한 눈물로 나를 저주하소서, 축복하소서, 비옵나니.
저 좋은 밤으로 얌전히 들어가지 마소서.
빛이 꺼져감에 격노하소서, 격노하소서.

The Force That Through the Green Fuse Drives the Flower

The force that through the green fuse drives the flower
Drives my green age; that blasts the roots of trees
Is my destroyer.
And I am dumb to tell the crooked rose
My youth is bent by the same wintry fever.

The force that drives the water through the rocks
Drives my red blood; that dries the mouthing streams
Turns mine to wax.
And I am dumb to mouth unto my veins
How at the mountain spring the same mouth sucks.

The hand that whirls the water in the pool
Stirs the quicksand; that ropes the blowing wind
Hauls my shroud sail.
And I am dumb to tell the hanging man
How of my clay is made the hangman's lime.

The lips of time leech to the fountain head;
Love drips and gathers, but the fallen blood
Shall calm her sores.
And I am dumb to tell a weather's wind
How time has ticked a heaven round the stars.

And I am dumb to tell the lover's tomb
How at my sheet goes the same crooked worm.

푸른 줄기 속으로 꽃을 모으는 힘은

푸른 줄기 속으로 꽃을 모는 힘은
나의 푸른 젊음을 모는 힘, 나무 뿌릴 시들게 하는 힘은
나를 파괴하는 힘.
나는 아연하여 비틀린 장미에게 말 못한다
나의 청춘도 또한 같은 冬熱에 시든다고.

바위 틈으로 물을 모는 힘은
나의 붉은 피를 모는 힘, 흐르는 개천물을 말리는 힘은
나의 피를 굳게 하는 힘.
나는 아연하여 내 혈관에 말 못한다
그 산샘을 같은 입이 빨고 있다고.

웅덩이의 물을 휘젓는 손이
유사를 움직이고, 부는 바람을 잡아 매는 손이
나의 수의의 돛을 끌어당긴다.
나는 아연하여 교수형 집행인에게 말 못한다
교수형 집행인의 석회는 나의 흙으로 만들어졌다고.

시간의 입술은 샘 머리에 붙어서 빨고,
사랑이 방울져 뭉친다, 그러나 흘린 피로
사랑의 상처는 진정하리라.
나는 아연하여 부는 바람에 말 못한다.
별들 주변에 시간이 천국을 새긴다고.

나는 아연하여 애인의 무덤에 말 못한다
내 침상에도 같은 나쁜 벙충이 기고 있다고.

In My Craft or Sullen Art

In my craft or sullen art
Exercised in the still night
When only the moon rages
And the lovers lie abed
With all their griefs in their arms
I labour by singing light
Not for ambition or bread
Or the strut and trade of charms
On the ivory stages
But for the common wages
Of their most secret heart.

Not for the proud man apart
From the raging moon I write
On these spindrift pages
Nor for the towering dead
With their nightingales and psalms
But for the lovers, their arms
Round the griefs of the ages,
Who pay no praise or wages
Nor heed my craft or art

나의 재간 지지부진한 기술로

고요한 밤
다만 달만이 불타고
애인들은 침대에 누워서
일체의 슬픔을 품안을 때 익힌,
나의 재간 지지부진한 기술로
나는 노래하는 빛 아래 노력한다.
야심에서도 아니고 빵을 위해서도 아니고
상아의 무대 위에서
뽐내며 돈벌이하고픈 매력에 끌려서도 아니다
다만 애인들의 가장 은밀한 마음이 주는
평범한 보수를 위해서다.
물보라 같은 종이 위에
내가 시를 쓰는 것은 불타는 달과는
동떨어진 오만한 자를 위해서도 아니고
나이팅게일이나 찬가로써 출중한
옛 사람들을 위함도 아니다.
대대의 슬픔을 품안는
애인들을 위해서다,
허나 그들은 내 재간 내 기술에
칭찬도 보수도 주지 않고 돌보지도 않누나.

Light Breaks Where No Sun Shines

Light breaks where no sun shines;
Where no sea runs, the waters of the heart
Push in their tides;
And, broken ghosts with glowworms in their heads,
The things of light
File through the flesh where no flesh decks the bones.

A candle in the thighs
Warms youth and seed and burns the seeds of age;
Where no seed stirs,
The fruit of man unwrinkles in the stars,
Bright as a fig;
Where no wax is, the candle shows its hairs.

Dawn breaks behind the eyes;
From poles of skull and toe the windy blood
Slides like a sea;
Nor fenced, nor staked, the gushers of the sky
Spout to the rod
Divining in a smile the oil of tears.

Night in the sockets rounds,
Like some pitch moon, the limit of the globes;
Day lights the bone;
Where no cold is, the skinning gales unpin
The winter's robes;
The film of spring is hanging from the lids.

해가 비치지 않는 곳에 빛이 터진다

해가 비치지 않는 곳에 빛이 터진다.
바다가 흐르지 않는 곳에서 심장의 물은
조류가 되어 밀고 들어오고,
머리에 반딧불 달린 깨어진 정령들,
빛나는 것들이
살이 뼈를 감싸고 있지 않은 살 속으로 열지어 지나간다.

허벅지 속에서 촛불이
젊음과 씨앗에 온기 주고, 나이의 씨앗들을 불태운다.
씨앗이 움직이지 않는 곳에서
인간의 열매는 별들 속에서 주름이 펴진다,
무화과처럼 찬란히.
밀랍이 없는 곳에서 촛불은 머리털을 보인다.

두 눈 뒤에서 새벽이 동튼다.
두개골과 발꿈치의 양극에서 바람 세찬 피가
바다처럼 흐른다.
울타리도 말뚝도 없이 하늘의 유정은
미소지으며 눈물과 기쁨을 점치는
지팡이에 따라 분출한다,

눈 구멍 속에서 밤이
새까만 달 같이 안구들의 경계를 돈다.
낮은 뼈를 비춘다,
추위가 없는 곳에서 살갗을 벗기는 바람이
겨울의 의상을 벗긴다.
봄의 영상이 눈까풀에 메달려 있다.

Light breaks on secret lots,
On tips of thought where thoughts smell in the rain;
When logics die,
The secret of the soil grows through the eye,
And blood jumps in the sun;
Above the waste allotments the dawn halts.

빛이 터진다, 비밀스런 운명에,
생각들이 비 속에서 냄새 맡는 사상의 비결로,
논리가 죽을 때,
흙의 비밀은 눈을 통하여 성장하고
피는 햇빛에서 뛴다,
황폐한 뭎 위에 새벽은 멈춘다.

This Bread I Break

This bread I break was once the oat,
This wine upon a foreign tree
Plunged in its fruit;
Man in the day or wine at night
Laid the crops low, broke the grape's joy.

Once in this time wine the summer blood
Knocked in the flesh that decked the vine,
Once in this bread
The oat was merry in the wind;
Man broke the sun, pulled the wind down.

This flesh you break, this blood you let
Make desolation in the vein,
Were oat and grape
Born of the sensual root and sap;
My wine you drink, my bread you snap.

내가 뜯는 이 빵은

내가 뜯는 이 빵은 전에 귀리였다.
이국 땅 나무에 매달렸던 이 포도주가
그 열매 속에 뛰어들었다.
낮에는 사람이 밤에는 바람이
그 곡식을 쓰러뜨렸고, 그 포도의 기쁨을 파괴했다.

한 때 이 포도주 속에서 여름 피가
덩굴을 장식한 살 속으로 쳐들어갔고,
한 때 이 빵 속에서
귀리는 바람 속에서 즐거웠는데,
인간은 태양을 부수고, 바람을 끌어내렸다.

네가 쪼개는 이 살, 네가 혈관 속에서
황량하게 만드는 이 피는
관능의 뿌리와 수석에서 자란,
귀리였고, 포도였다.
내 포도주를 네가 마시고, 내 빵을 네가 물어뜯는다.

Philip Larkin (1922-1985)

On August 9, 1922, Philip Larkin was born in Coventry, England. He attended St. John's College, Oxford. His first book of poetry, *The North Ship*, was published in 1945 and, though not particularly strong on its own, is notable insofar as certain passages foreshadow the unique sensibility and maturity that characterizes his later work.

In 1946, Larkin discovered the poetry of Thomas Hardy and became a great admirer of his poetry, learning from Hardy how to make the commonplace and often dreary details of his life the basis for extremely tough, unsparing, and memorable poems. With his second volume of poetry, *The Less Deceived* (1955), Larkin became the preeminent poet of his generation, and a leading voice of what came to be called "The Movement," a group of young English writers who rejected the prevailing fashion for neo-Romantic writing in the style of Yeats and Dylan Thomas. Like Hardy, Larkin focused on intense personal emotion but strictly avoided sentimentality or self-pity.

In 1964, he confirmed his reputation as a major poet with the publication of *The Whitsun Weddings*, and again in 1974 with *High Windows*: collections whose searing, often mocking, wit does not conceal the poet's dark vision and underlying obsession with universal themes of mortality, love, and human solitude. Deeply anti-social and a great lover and published critic of American jazz, Larkin never married and worked as a librarian in the provincial city of Hull, where he died on December 2, 1985.

Days

What are days for?
Days are where we live.
They come, they wake us
Time and time over.
They are to be happy in:
Where can we live but days?

Ah, solving that question
Brings the priest and the doctor
In their long coats
Running over the fields.

나날

나날이 왜 있지?
나날은 우리 사는 곳에 있다.
그것들 온다, 그것들 우리를 깨운다
거듭거듭.
그것들 있다 그 안에서 행복하려고:
나날 말고 우리가 어디서 살 수 있나?

아, 그 문제를 푸는 일
초래하지 사제와 의사
긴 옷 차림의,
들판 가득.

Deceptions

"Of course I was drugged, and so heavily I did not regain consciousness until the next morning. I was horrified to discover that I had been ruined, and for some days I was inconsolable,
and cried like a child to be killed or sent back to my aunt."

—Mayhew, London Labour and the London Poor

Even so distant, I can taste the grief,
Bitter and sharp with stalks, he made you gulp.
The sun's occasional print, the brisk brief
Worry of wheels along the street outside
Where bridal London bows the other way,
And light, unanswerable and tall and wide,
Forbids the scar to heal, and drives
Shame out of hiding. All the unhurried day,
Your mind lay open like a drawer of knives.

Slums, years, have buried you. I would not dare
Console you if I could. What can be said,
Except that suffering is exact, but where
Desire takes charge, readings will grow erratic?
For you would hardly care
That you were less deceived, out on that bed,
Than he was, stumbling up the breathless stair
To burst into fulfillment's desolate attic.

속임수들

"물론 나는 마약에 취한 상태였고, 너무도 심하여 다음 날 아침까지
의식을 되찾지 못했을 정도였다. 망가졌다는 것을 알게 된 나는 소름이
끼쳤고, 며칠 동안 어떤 위로의 말도 소용이 없었고, 아이처럼 울었다.
곧
살해당하거나 내 이모에게 다시 돌려보내지기라도 할 것처럼."

—메이휴, 런던 노동과 런던의 가난한 사람들

그토록 멀더라도, 나는 느낄 수 있다 그 슬픔의 맛을,
줄기 쓰라리고 날카로운 그것을, 그가 그대에게 꿀꺽꿀꺽 삼키게 했군.
태양의 가끔가끔 인쇄, 빠르고 짧은
근심, 바퀴들의, 거리를 따라 바깥
결혼식의 런던이 다른 쪽 보고 절하는 곳으로 굴러가는,
그리고 빛, 반박할 수 없고 키 크고 너비 넓은,
그것이 금지한다 상처 낫는 것을, 그리고 몰아낸다
치욕을 치욕의 은신처에서. 느긋한 하루 온종일
그대 마음 열려 있다 칼을 넣어두는 서랍처럼.

빈민가, 세월, 이 그대를 묻었다. 나는 감히
그대를 위로하지 않을 테다 그럴 수 있단들. 무슨 말을 하겠나,
고통은 정확하다, 그러나
욕망이 폭주하면, 독서가 변덕스러워지리라는 말 말고는?
왜냐면 그대한테는 별 상관이 없을 터
그대가 덜 속았다는 게, 그 노천 침대에서.
누구긴, 숨가쁜 계단을 발 헛디디며 올라
충족의 적막한 다락으로 뛰어들던 그보다 덜 말이지.

MCMXIV(1914)

Those long uneven lines
Standing as patiently
As if they were stretched outside
The Oval or Villa Park,
The crowns of hats, the sun
On moustached archaic faces
Grinning as if it were all
An August Bank Holiday lark;

And the shut shops, the bleached
Established names on the sunblinds,
The farthings and sovereigns,
And dark-clothed children at play
Called after kings and queens,
The tin advertisements
For cocoa and twist, and the pubs
Wide open all day;

And the countryside not caring:
The place-names all hazed over
With flowering grasses, and fields
Shadowing Domesday lines
Under wheat's restless silence;
The differently-dressed servants
With tiny rooms in huge houses,
The dust behind limousines;

1914년

그 길고 울퉁불퉁한 줄들,
끈기 있게 서 있는 것이
마치 그들 이어진 게
미국 대통령 집무실이나 빌라 파크 바깥인 것처럼,
왕관 같은 모자들, 태양,
콧수염 고졸풍 얼굴들 위에
얼굴들 씨익 웃는 게 마치 모두
8월 공휴일 장난치며 떠들어댄다는 듯;

그리고 닫힌 가게들, 바래진
자리 잡은 이름, 차양들 위에,
옛 4분의 1페니짜리 파딩 동전과 일 파운드짜리 소브린 금화들,
그리고 검은 옷 아이들, 노는,
왕과 왕비들 이름을 따서 이름 지어진,
주석 광고판,
코코아 마시고 트위스트 추는, 그리고 선술집
하루 종일 활짝 열린;

그리고 시골 지역, 보살핌 없는:
지명들, 모두 흐릿해진
꽃 피우는 풀들 때문이지, 그리고 들판들,
소백의 가만히 못 있는 침묵 아래
최후 심판일 늘어선 줄들에 그늘 드리우는;
복장이 서로 다른 하인들,
거대한 저택에 자그만 방을 갖고 있는,
리무진 뒤 먼지;

Never such innocence,
Never before or since,
As changed itself to past
Without a word – the men
Leaving the gardens tidy,
The thousands of marriages,
Lasting a little while longer:
Never such innocence again.

이런 순수 한 번도,
그전에도 그이래로도,
스스로 과거화한 적 없었다
말 한마디 없이—사내들
정원을 깔끔하게 두지,
수천의 결혼들
조금 더 오래가지:
이런 순수 다시 없어라.

This Be the Verse

They fuck you up, your mum and dad.
　They may not mean to, but they do.
They fill you with the faults they had
　And add some extra, just for you.

But they were fucked up in their turn
　By fools in old-style hats and coats,
Who half the time were soppy-stern
　And half at one another's throats.

Man hands on misery to man.
　It deepens like a coastal shelf.
Get out as early as you can,
　And don't have any kids yourself.

이것 시이기를

그들이 조진다, 네 신세를. 네 엄마와 아빠 말이다.
　본의는 아닐지 모르나, 그들이 정말 그런다.
그들이 너를 채운다 그들이 지닌 결점들로
　그리고 더한다 모종의 추가. 바로 너를 위해서.

그러나 그들은 그들대로 신세 조짐당한 신세,
　구식 모자와 외투 차림 바보들에 의해,
시간의 반은 몹시 감상적이고
　반은 서로의 멱살을 쥐던 것들이지.

사람이 건넨다 비참을 사람에게.
　그것 깊어진다 해변의 선반 모양 지층처럼.
빠져나가라 될 수 있는 대로 일찍,
　그리고 너 자신 아이 따위 하나도 갖지 말아라.

Toads

Why should I let the toad work
    Squat on my life?
Can't I use my wit as a pitchfork
    And drive the brute off?

Six days of the week it soils
    With its sickening poison -
Just for paying a few bills!
    That's out of proportion.

Lots of folk live on their wits:
    Lecturers, lispers,
Losels, loblolly-men, louts-
    They don't end as paupers;

Lots of folk live up lanes
    With fires in a bucket,
Eat windfalls and tinned sardines-
    they seem to like it.

Their nippers have got bare feet,
    Their unspeakable wives
Are skinny as whippets - and yet
    No one actually starves.

Ah, were I courageous enough
    To shout Stuff your pension!
But I know, all too well, that's the stuff
    That dreams are made on:

두꺼비

왜 내가 두꺼비 같은 일을 하게 하며
　　내 인생에 쪼그리고 앉아 있게 해야 하나?
내 기지를 발휘해 갈퀴처럼 사용해서
　　그 짐승을 몰아 낼 수는 없을까?

일주일에 6일은 그 두꺼비가
　　역겹게 만드는 독으로 더럽힌다.
얼마 안 되는 계산서를 지불하려고!
　　전혀 합당하지 않은 비율이다.

많은 사람들은 그들의 기지로 살아간다.
　　강연자들, 가식적인 자들
건달들, 광대 같은 자들, 사기꾼들
　　그렇지만 그들은 가난뱅이로 끝나지 않는다.

많은 사람들은 길가에서 살아간다.
　　통 안에 불을 지피고,
떨어진 과일과 정어리 통조림을 먹는다.
　　그들은 그것을 괜찮게 여겨 보인다.

그들의 어린아이들은 맨발이고,
　　그들의 말로 형언하기 어려운 부인들은
휘펫처럼 비쩍 말랐다. 그래도
　　아무도 실제로는 굶어죽을 지경은 아니다.

아, 내가 '하찮은 연금 따위!'라고 소리칠 정도로
　　충분히 용기가 있었다면
그러나 나는 안다, 너무나 잘, 이것이
　　꿈이 만들어 지는 재료가 됨을

For something sufficiently toad-like
    Squats in me, too;
Its hunkers are heavy as hard luck,
    And cold as snow,

And will never allow me to blarney
    My way of getting
The fame and the girl and the money
    All at one sitting.

I don't say, one bodies the other
    One's spiritual truth;
But I do say it's hard to lose either,
    When you have both.

충분히 두꺼비 같은 그 어떤 것이
　　내안에도 존재하기 때문에,
그것의 궁둥이가 액운과도 같이 무겁고,
　　눈과 같이 차갑다

그리고 나로 하여금 허락하지 않을 것이다.
　　유명세, 여자, 그리고 돈
이 모든 것을 한번에
　　아첨 따위를 해서 획득하게끔

나는 어느 한 가지 것이 나머지 것의
　　정신적 진실을 형태화 한다고 말하는 것은 아니다.
그러나 어느 쪽도 잃기란 어려운 것이라 말하는 것이다.
　　당신이 둘 다를 갖고 있을 때는

Wedding-Wind

The wind blew all my wedding-day,
And my wedding-night was the night of the high wind;
And a stable door was banging, again and again,
That he must go and shut it, leaving me
Stupid in candlelight, hearing rain,
Seeing my face in the twisted candlestick,
Yet seeing nothing. When he came back
He said the horses were restless, and I was sad
That any man or beast that night should lack
The happiness I had.

Now in the day
All's ravelled under the sun by the wind's blowing.
He has gone to look at the floods, and I
Carry a chipped pail to the chicken-run,
Set it down, and stare. All is the wind
Hunting through clouds and forests, thrashing
My apron and the hanging cloths on the line.
Can it be borne, this bodying-forth by wind
Of joy my actions turn on, like a thread
Carrying beads? Shall I be let to sleep
Now this perpetual morning shares my bed?
Can even death dry up
These new delighted lakes, conclude
Our kneeling as cattle by all-generous waters?

결혼식날 바람

내 결혼식날 진종일 바람이 불었다,
그리고 결혼날 밤은 바람이 심하게 분 밤이었다.
마굿간 문이 연달아 탕탕거려,
그는 나가서 문을 닫아야 했고, 나는
빗 소리 들으며 멍청히 촛불 밑에 있어야 했다,
뒤틀린 촛대에 내 얼굴이 보였지만
아무것도 눈에 들어오지 않았다. 그는 돌아와서
말들이 불안해한다고 말했지만, 나는 슬펐다,
그날 밤 사람이고 짐승이고 누구 하나
내가 가진 행복을 갖지 못한 것이.

이제 낮이 되니
모든 것이 바람으로 헝클어진 채 햇빛에 드러났다.
그는 홍수난 것을 보러 나갔고, 나는
귀 떨어진 물통을 들고 닭 우리로 가서
그것을 놓고 들여다 본다. 바람이 온통
구름 사이 숲 사이를 뒤지고, 줄에 걸린
나의 에이프런과 보자기를 휘갈긴다.
이렇게까지 될 수 있을까 — 바람이
내 행동이 불붙인 기쁨을 염주 꿴 실처럼
확실한 것으로 만들어 낼 수 있을까. 잠이 들 것인가,
영원한 아침이 내 침상에 같이 누워 있는데.
죽음이 이 새로운 즐거움의 호수를 말려버리고
아주 너그러운 물가에서 소들처럼 무릎 꿇고 있는
우리에게 종말을 가져오는 일이 있을까.

Seamus Heaney (1939-2013)

Seamus Heaney was born on April 13, 1939, in Castledawson, County Derry, Northern Ireland. He earned a teacher's certificate in English at St. Joseph's College in Belfast and in 1963 took a position as a lecturer in English at that school. While at St. Joseph's he began to write, joining a poetry workshop with Derek Mahon, Michael Longley, and others under the guidance of Philip Hobsbaum. In 1965 he married Marie Devlin, and the following year he published *Death of a Naturalist* (1966).

He produced numerous collections of poetry, including *Human Chain* (2010), *District and Circle* (2006), *Opened Ground* (1999), which was named a New York Times Notable Book of the Year; *The Spirit Level* (1996); *Selected Poems* 1966–1987 (1990); and *Sweeney Astray* (1983). He also wrote several volumes of criticism, including *The Redress of Poetry* (1995), and of translation, including *Beowulf* (2000), which won the Whitbread Book of the Year Award.

Some of Heaney's poetry has for its theme the struggle between Protestants and Catholics in Northern Ireland, which he observes from an independent and personal point of view. Like many Irish poets in the twentieth century, he also takes Ireland itself for one of his subjects—the nature of the land, its tragic history, and the character and ways of life of its people. But although he is firmly identified with Ireland, Heaney, like Yeats, also transcends this national identification. Heaney's poetry is not personal or idyllic, for he is deeply sensitive to the darker side of human existence; but he shows a great deal of compassion, affection, humor, and pleasure, particularly in the rural and earthy things.

Seamus Heaney passed away in Dublin, Ireland, on August 30, 2013. He was seventy-four.

A Drink of Water

She came every morning to draw water
Like an old bat staggering up the field:
The pump's whooping cough, the bucket's clatter
And slow diminuendo as it filled,
Announced her. I recall
Her her grey apron, the pocked white enamel
Of the brimming bucket, and the treble
Creak of her voice like the pump's handle.
Nights when a full moon lifted past her gable
It fell back through her window and would lie
Into the water set out on the table.
Where I have dipped to drink again, to be
Faithful to the admonishment on her cup,
Remember the Giver fading off the lip.

물 한모금

늙은 박쥐 한 마리가 비틀거리며 들판으로 날아오듯이
그녀는 매일 아침 물을 뜨러 왔다.
쿨룩쿨룩 기침하는 듯한 펌프 소리, 덜그럭 거리는 바켓 소리.
그리고 찰수록 서서이 작아지는 물 소리 등으로
그녀가 와 있는 것을 알 수 있었다. 나는 머리에 그린다 —
그녀의 회색 에이프런과, 물이 가득 찬
바켓의 너덜너덜한 하얀 에나멜과, 펌프 손잡이 같이
고음으로 끽끽거리는 그녀의 목소리를.
보름달이 그녀의 집 처마를 지나 높이 EJ 있는 밤이면 밤마다
달빛이 그녀의 창문으로 스며들어
식탁 위에 놓인 물잔 속으로 비춰들었다.
나는 그 물을 다시 떠서 한 모금 마시고
그녀의 물잔에 쓰여진 '준 사람을 잊지 말라'는
교훈을 지키려 하였으나 글씨가 컵 가장자리에서 사라지고 있었다.

Digging

Between my finger and my thumb
The squat pen rests; snug as a gun.

Under my window, a clean rasping sound
When the spade sinks into gravelly ground:
My father, digging. I look down

Till his straining rump among the flowerbeds
Bends low, comes up twenty years away
Stooping in rhythm through potato drills
Where he was digging.

The coarse boot nestled on the lug, the shaft
Against the inside knee was levered firmly.
He rooted out tall tops, buried the bright edge deep
To scatter new potatoes that we picked,
Loving their cool hardness in our hands.

By God, the old man could handle a spade.
Just like his old man.

My grandfather cut more turf in a day
Than any other man on Toner's bog.
Once I carried him milk in a bottle
Corked sloppily with paper. He straightened up
To drink it, then fell to right away
Nicking and slicing neatly, heaving sods
Over his shoulder, going down and down
For the good turf. Digging.

땅 파기

내 손가락과 엄지 사이에
뭉툭한 펜이 놓여있다; 총처럼 믿음직하게.

창문 밑에서는 싹싹 소리가 맑게 들린다.
삽이 자갈 땅을 파고 든다,
아버지가 땅을 파고, 나는 내려다 본다.

화단에서 아버지가 팽팽한 엉덩이를
낮게 구부리고 이십년 전 그 옛날
감자밭 이랑 사이에서 일정하게 허리를 굽혔다 폈다
그 분이 땅을 파는 모습이 눈에 들어온다.

투박한 장화를 보습에 올려놓고 삽자루를
무릎 안쪽에 대어 단단한 힘을 가한다.
아버지는 키 큰 줄기를 뽑아내고 빛나는 삽날을
깊숙이 박고 햇감자를 들추어 털어낸다,
양손에 그 서늘한 단단한 감촉을 즐기며.

정말로, 아버지는 삽질을 잘 하셨다.
아버지의 아버지처럼.

조부께서는 토너 늪지에서 하루에
어느 누구보다도 토탄을 더 많이 잘라내셨다.
언젠가 나는 허술하게 종이로 마개한 물병에
우유를 갖다 드렸다. 조부는 허리를 펴
그것을 마시고는 바로 또 허리를 구부리고
뗏장에 눈금을 그어 정연하게 잘라냈다.
흙을 어깨 너머로 던지면서
좋은 토탄을 찾아 파고 또 팠다.

The cold smell of potato mould, the squelch and slap
Of soggy peat, the curt cuts of an edge
Through living roots awaken in my head.
But I've no spade to follow men like them.

Between my finger and my thumb
The squat pen rests.
I'll dig with it.

감자밭의 찬 흙냄새, 축축한 토탄의 물렁물렁하고
질퍽한 모양새, 살아있는 뿌리를 거칠게 자른
날카로운 삽자국 등이 머리에 되살아난다.
그러나 나는 그분들의 뒤를 따를 삽을 갖고 있지 않다.

손가락과 엄지 사이에
뭉툭한 펜이 놓여 있다.
나는 이것으로 파리라.

Follower

My father worked with a horse-plough,
His shoulders globed like a full sail strung
Between the shafts and the furrow.
The horse strained at his clicking tongue.

An expert. He would set the wing
And fit the bright steel-pointed sock.
The sod rolled over without breaking.
At the headrig, with a single pluck

Of reins, the sweating team turned round
And back into the land. His eye
Narrowed and angled at the ground,
Mapping the furrow exactly.

I stumbled in his hob-nailed wake,
Fell sometimes on the polished sod;
Sometimes he rode me on his back
Dipping and rising to his plod.

I wanted to grow up and plough,
To close one eye, stiffen my arm.
All I ever did was follow
In his broad shadow round the farm.

I was a nuisance, tripping, falling,
Yapping always. But today
It is my father who keeps stumbling
Behind me, and will not go away.

뒤 따르는 사람

아버지는 말이 끄는 쟁기로 일을 하셨다.
두 어깨는 바람이 꽉 찬 돛폭 같았다,
쟁기 손잡이와 밭이랑 사이에 묶여 있는.
말들은 아버지의 혀 차는 소리에 긴장하곤 했다.

전문가셨다. 아버지는 쟁기 날개를 고정시키고
번쩍이는 강철 뾰족 보습을 맞추셨다.
흙은 부서지지 않고 갈려 엎어졌고,
이랑 머리에서 고삐를 한 번 잡아당기자

말들은 땀을 흘리며 뒤로 돌아
다시 밭으로 들어간다. 아버지의 눈은
가늘게 뜨고 땅을 노려보면서
이랑을 정확히 구획지어 가셨다.

나는 아버지의 징 박은 구두 자국에 고꾸라지면서
때로는 번들번들한 흙 위에 자빠지기도 했다.
때론 아버지가 나를 등에 업고서 천천히
발을 옮기셨다, 그에 맞춰 솟아올랐다, 가라앉았다 하면서.

나는 커서 쟁기질 하고 싶었다,
한 눈을 감고 팔을 빳빳하게 뻗치고서.
내가 할 수 있는 일이란 고작 따라가는 것 뿐이었다,
농장을 돌아 아버지의 커다란 그림자 속에서.

나는 한낱 귀찮은 존재였다, 깡충깡충 뛰면서, 자빠지면서
늘 재재거리면서. 그러나 오늘은
내 뒤에서 고꾸라지면서 내게
바싹 따라붙는 것은 아버지이시다.

Hercules and Antaeus

Sky-born and royal,
snake-choker, dung-heaver,
his mind big with golden apples,
his future hung with trophies,

Hercules has the measure
of resistance and black powers
feeding off the territory.
Antaeus, the mould-hugger,

is weaned at last:
a fall was a renewal
but now he is raised up-
the challenger's intelligence

is a spur of light,
a blue prong graiping him
out of his element
into a dream of loss

and origins-the cradling dark,
the river-veins, the secret gullies
of his strength,
the hatching grounds

of cave and souterrain,
he has bequeathed it all
to elegists. Balor will die
and Byrthnoth and Sitting Bull.

헤르쿨레스와 안타이오스

하늘에서 태어나고 왕족인,
뱀을 목 졸라 죽인 자, 똥을 들어올린 자.
그의 마음 황금의 사과들로 거창하고,
그의 미래 전리품들이 매달려 있는.

헤라클레스는 갖고 있다 수단.
저항 수단과 검은 능력,
영역을 모조리 간파하는 능력을.
안타이오스, 거푸집을 껴안는 자,

가 마침내 젖을 떼인다:
추락이 재생이었으나
이제 그는 높이 들렸다—
도전자의 지능

은 빛의 박차,
하늘색 갈퀴가 그를 그의
원소 바깥으로 긁어내고 긁어 들인다
어떤 꿈, 상실과

기원의 꿈속으로—요람인 어둠,
강-정맥, 은밀한 협곡,
그의 힘의,
부화시키는 땅.

동굴과 지하은신처의.
그는 물려주었다 그 모든 것을
엘레지 시인들에게. 발로르는 죽을 것이다
비르트노트와 앉은 소도.

Hercules lifts his arms
in a remorawlwaa V,
his triumph unassailed
by the powers he has shaken,

and lifts and banks Antaeus
high as a profiled ridge,
a sleeping giant,
pap for the dispossessed.

헤라클레스가 두 팔을 올린다.
냉혹한 V자로.
그의 승리 그가 흔들어놓은 세력에
끄떡없는 채.

그리고 올리고 쌓는다 안타이오스를
옆모습 윤곽의 산마루처럼 높게.
잠든 거인,
박탈당한 자들을 위한 젖꼭지 언덕.

Mother of the Groom

What she remembers
Is his glistening back
In the bath, his small boots
In the ring of boots at her feet.

Hands in her voided lap,
She hears a daughter welcomed.
It's as if he kicked when lifted
And slipped her soapy hold.

Once soap would ease off
The wedding ring
That's bedded forever now
In her clapping hand.

신랑의 어머니

그녀가 기억하는 것은
그의 반짝이는 등.
욕조 속의, 그의 작은 장화.
그녀 발아래 빙 둘러앉은 장화들 속의.

허전해진 무릎에 두 손을 두고.
그녀는 듣는다. 딸애 환영받는 소리.
그것은 마치 위로 들려진 그가 발길질을 하고
그녀의 비누 미끈미끈한 손아귀를 미끄러져 나간 것 같다.

한번은 비누가 쉽게 빼주었지
결혼반지를
이제는 그것이 영원한 지층 이루었다
손뼉 치는 그녀 손에.

Punishment

I can feel the tug
of the halter at the nape
of her neck, the wind
on her naked front.

It blows her nipples
to amber beads,
it shakes the frail rigging
of her ribs.

I can see her drowned
body in the bog,
the weighing stone,
the floating rods and boughs.

Under which at first
she was a barked sapling
that is dug up
oak-bone, brain-firkin:

her shaved head
like a stubble of black corn,
her blindfold a soiled bandage,
her noose a ring

to store
the memories of love.
Little aduleress,
before they punished you

형벌

밧줄이 그녀의 목덜미를
조이고 바람이
그녀의 맨살 앞가슴에
와닿는 것이 느껴진다.

바람은 그녀의 젖꼭지를
호박색 염주로 변색시키고,
그 바람에 그녀의 갈비뼈의
연약한 용마루가 흔들린다.

늪 속 물에 잠긴
그녀의 시체가 보일 것 같다.
시신을 가라앉히는 돌,
둥둥 떠있는 작은 나뭇가지와 큰 가지.

늪 속에서 그녀는 처음엔
한낱 껍질 벗겨진 어린 나무였다.
그것이 이제 파올려지니
뼈는 오크나무, 머리는 물통.

빡빡 깎인 그녀의 머리는
검은 보리밭 그루터기 같고,
흙묻은 붕대에 눈이 가려지고
목에 감긴 밧줄은

사랑의 추억을
간직한 반지.
너에게 형벌이 가해지기 전
너는 어린 간통녀,

you were flaxen-haired,
undernourished, and your
tar-black face was beautiful.
My poor scapegoat,

I almost love you
but would have case, I know,
the stones of silence.
I am the artful voyeur

of your brain's exposed
and darkened combs,
your muscles' webbing
and all your numbered bones:

I who have stood dumb
when your betraying sisters,
cauled in tar,
wept by the railings,

who would connive
in civilized outrage
yet understand the exact
and tribal, intimate revenge.

삼단 같은 머리를 하고
못 먹어 야위고,
새까만 얼굴은 고왔다.
나의 가엾은 희생양.

나는 너를 거의 사랑한다.
그러나 침묵의 돌을
던지고자 했을 것이다.
나는 교활한 엿보기 취미자이다.

너의 노출된 시커먼
벌집 같은 두뇌,
거미줄 같은 근육,
그리고 너의 하나하나 셀 수 있는 뼈대를 엿보는 나는.

너의 배반자 친구들이
타르를 뒤집어 쓰고
가드레일 가에서 울고 있을 때에도
입 다물고 서있던 나.

문명화된 난폭을
보고도 못본 체 외면하면서도, 그 엄격한
부족간의 사사로운 보복은
용인하는 나.

Carol Ann Duffy (1955-)

On December 23, 1955, Carol Ann Duffy was born in Glasgow, Scotland to Mary Black and Frank Duffy, both of Irish Catholic descent. Together with her four younger brothers, she was raised in Staffordshire in the West Midlands of England where her father worked as a fitter with English Electric.

She received a degree in philosophy from Liverpool University in 1977. Her first job was writing for television shows, followed by a C. Day Lewis Fellowship to work as a writer-in-residence in East End schools of London from 1982 and 1984.

Duffy's books of poetry include: *New & Collected Poetry for Children* (2009); *Rapture* (2006); *Selected Poems* (2004); *Feminine Gospels* (2002); and *The World's Wife* (2000), a collection of poetic retellings voiced by the wives of the famous and infamous. Her earlier volumes include: *Mean Time* (1993), which won the Whitbread Poetry Award and the Forward Poetry Prize; *The Other Country* (1990); *Selling Manhattan* (1987), winner of a Somerset Maugham Award; and her first collection, *Standing Female Nude* (1985), for which she received a Scottish Arts Council Award.

Dramatic characters and narratives, voiced with a sharp edge of wit and social critique, characterize Duffy's early work, while her recent collections have wrestled more directly with dark and tangled themes of love. Writing for *The Independent*, Ruth Padel called *Rapture* "a superb demonstration of … Duffy's formidably inventive artistry, her dedication to the craft and tradition of poetry, and above all the love poem."

In addition to poetry, Duffy has edited numerous anthologies, authored several critically-acclaimed plays and children's books, and has collaborated with the singer and composer Eliana Tomkins on a series of jazz performances. Her books for children include *The Hat* (2007), *The Oldest Girl in the World* (2000), and *Meeting Midnight* (1999).

Duffy was the longtime editor of the poetry magazine *Ambit*, and has been a frequent reviewer and critic for many publications, including *The Guardian*. She lives in Manchester and is the Creative Director of the Writing School at Manchester Metropolitan University. Duffy was appointed as Britain's Poet Laureate on May 1, 2009, becoming both the first woman and the first openly lesbian poet to hold the position in its more than 300 year history.

Anne Hathaway

'Item I gyve unto my wief my second best bed…'
(from Shakespeare's will)

The bed we loved in was a spinning world
of forests, castles, torchlight, cliff-tops, seas
where he would dive for pearls. My lover's words
were shooting stars which fell to earth as kisses
on these lips; my body now a softer rhyme
to his, now echo, assonance; his touch
a verb dancing in the centre of a noun.
Some nights I dreamed he'd written me, the bed
a page beneath his writer's hands. Romance
and drama played by touch, by scent, by taste.
In the other bed, the best, our guests dozed on,
dribbling their prose. My living laughing love –
I hold him in the casket of my widow's head
as he held me upon that next best bed.

앤 해서웨이

'내 아내에게 남긴 차상의 침대...'
(셰익스피어의 유서에서)

우리가 사랑을 나누었던 침대는 숲과 성과
횃불과 벼랑 끝, 그리고 그가 진주를 찾아 잠수할
수도 있을 바다로 만들어진 빙빙 도는 세계. 내 연인의
말은 이 입술에 닿을 키스처럼 땅에 떨어질
별똥별. 내 몸은 지금 그의 몸에 맞춰진 부드러운
운율, 바로 메아리, 그리고 유음. 그의 애무는
명사 한가운데에서 춤추는 동사.
그가 나를 새기고 있다고 꿈꾼 어떤 밤에 그 침대는
집필하는 그의 손아래에 있는 한 장의 종이. 어루만짐으로,
냄새로, 맛으로 연출된 로맨스와 드라마.
다른 최상의 침대에서 우리 손님들은 그들의 산문을
질질 흘리며 졸고 있고. 나의 살아 있는 즐거운 사랑--
그가 차상의 침대에서 나를 쥘 때처럼
나는 미망인인 내 머리 상자에 그를 붙들어 맨다.

Money Talks

I am the authentic language of suffering. My cold, gold eye
does not blink. Mister, you want nice time? No problem.
I say, *Screw You.* I buy and sell the world. I got
Midas touch, turn bread to hard cash. My million tills
sing through the night, my shining mad machines.
I stink and accumulate. *Do you fancy me, lady? Really?*

See me pass through the eye of a needle! Whoopee,
I cut Time dead with my sleek facelift. I travel
faster than $-sound. Don't give me away; after all, no one
can eat me. Honey, I'm a jealous God, $-stammering
my one commandment on the calculator. *Love me.*
Under your fingernails I smile up with my black grin.

Don't let my oily manner bother you, Sir, I'll get you
a taxi, get you a limousine. I know a place
where it's raining dollar bills. I got any currency
you want, women and gigolos, metal tuxedos. The party
is one long gold-toothed scream. Have a good day. I am
the big bombs, sighing in their thick lead sheaths OK.

돈이 말한다

나는 고통의 진정한 언어이다. 나의 차가운, 황금 눈동자는
깜작하지도 않는다. 아저씨, 당신은 즐거운 시간을 원하나요? 아무 문
제없죠.
나는 *엿 먹으라*고 말한다. 나는 세상을 사고판다. 나는
미다스의 손을 가지고 있어서, 빵을 단단한 현금으로 바꾼다. 내 수많은
계산기들은
밤새 노래를 한다, 내 빛나는 미치도록 좋아하는 돈궤들.
나는 악취를 풍기고 축척된다. *나에게 호감이 있나, 아가씨? 정말?*

내가 바늘구멍을 통과하는 것을 봐! 야호,
나는 매끈하게 성형한 얼굴로 시간을 못 본 척 하지. 나는
달러 소리보다 더 빠르게 움직이지. 나를 헐값에 넘기지 마; 결국
아무도 나를 망가뜨릴 수 없어. 아가씨, 나는 질투의 신이지, 내 유일한
계명은 계산기에서 달러-더듬거리기. *나를 사랑해줘.*
나는 네 손톱 밑에서 사악한 웃음을 지어보이지.

내가 사근사근한 게 문제가 없죠, 아저씨, 택시를
잡아줄까요, 리무진으로요. 달라 지폐가
비오는 듯 내리는 곳을 알아요. 원하는 통화,
여자와 기둥 서방, 금속 턱시도 다 준비되죠. 파티는
금빛으로 만연한 즐거움이죠. 즐겁게 보내요. 그래, 나는
두꺼운 납 덮개 속에서 살랑대고 있는 거대한 폭탄이라고.

Standing Female Nude

Six hours like this for a few francs.
Belly nipple arse in the window light,
he drains the color from me. Further to the right,
Madame. And do try to be still.
I shall be represented analytically and hung
in great museums. The bourgeoisie will coo
at such an image of a river-whore. They call it Art.

Maybe. He is concerned with volume, space.
I with the next meal. You're getting thin,
Madame, this is not good. My breasts hang
slightly low, the studio is cold. In the tea-leaves
I can see the Queen of England gazing
on my shape. Magnificent, she murmurs,
moving on. It makes me laugh. His name

is Georges. They tell me he's a genius.
There are times he does not concentrate
and stiffens for my warmth.
He possesses me on canvas as he dips the brush
repeatedly into the paint. Little man,
you've not the money for the arts I sell.
Both poor, we make our living how we can.
I ask him Why do you do this? Because
I have to. There's no choice. Don't talk.
My smile confuses him. These artists
take themselves too seriously. At night I fill myself
with wine and dance around the bars. When it's finished
he shows me proudly, lights a cigarette. I say
Twelve francs and get my shawl. It does not look like me.

서 있는 여성 누드

몇 푼을 받고 이렇게 여섯 시간이나.
창틀 사이 햇살을 받는 배 젖꼭지 엉덩이
그가 나에게서 색채를 앗아갔다. 오른 쪽으로 조금만,
그리고 좀 가만 있어봐.
나는 분석적으로 그려져 커다란
미술관에 걸리겠지. 부르주아들이 이런 강변의 창녀 같은
이미지를 보며 논란 듯 바라볼 거야. 명작이라고 하면서.

아마도. 그는 볼륨과 공간에 관심이 있다.
나는 다음 끼니에 관심이 있고. 부인, 점점 마르는 것
같아요. 좋지 않은데요. 내 가슴은 조금
아래로 쳐져 있다. 방이 춥다. 차 잎사귀 사이에서
영국 여왕이 내 몸을 물끄러미 바라보고 있는
모습을 볼 수 있다. 굉장하군요. 여왕이 천천히 몸을
움직이면서 중얼거린다. 그게 나를 웃긴다. 그의 이름은

조지이다. 사람들은 나에게 그가 천재라고 말한다.
그가 집중하지 않고 내 몸의 따뜻함 때문에
뻣뻣하게 굳어지는 때도 있다.
그는 붓을 그림 속에 여러 번 적시면서 나를
소유한다. 조그만 남자.
너는 내가 파는 예술을 살 돈이 없어.
우리 둘 가난하여 할 수 있는 방식으로 생계를 잇지.
그에게 묻는다. 왜 이런 일을 하세요? 왜냐하면
해야만 하니까. 선택의 여지가 없어. 말하지 마.
내 웃음이 그를 혼란스럽게 한다. 예술가들이라는 사람들은
자신을 너무 진지하게 생각하지. 밤이면 나는 술집
주변을 돌며 술과 춤으로 채우는데. 그림이 다 끝나면 그는
자랑하듯 보여주며 담배를 피워 문다. 나는 숄을 두르면서
12프랑이에요 라고 말한다. 그건 나와 닮지 않았다.

Translating the English, 1989

'...and much of the poetry, alas, is lost in translation...'

Welcome to my country! We have here Edwina Currie
and The Sun newspaper. Much excitement.
Also the weather has been most improving
even in February. Daffodils. (Wordsworth. Up North.) If you like
Shakespeare or even Opera we have too the Black Market.
For two hundred quids we are talking Les Miserables,
nods being as good as winks. Don't eat the eggs.
Wheel-clamp. Dogs. Vagrants. A tour of our wonderful
capital city is not to be missed. The Fergie,
The Princess Di and the football hooligan, truly you will
like it here, Squire. Also we can be talking crack, smack
and Carling Black Label if we are so inclined. Don't
drink the H2O. All very proud we now have
a green Prime Minister. What colour yours? Binbags.
You will be knowing of Charles Dickens and Terry Wogan
and Scotland. All this can be arranged for cash no questions.
Ireland not on. Fish and chips and the Official Secrets Act
second to none. Here we go. We are liking
a smashing good time like estate agents and Neighbours,
also Brookside for we are allowed four Channels.
How many you have? Last night of Proms. Andrew
Lloyd-Webber. Jeffrey Archer. Plenty culture you will be agreeing.
Also history and buildings. The Houses of Lords. Docklands.
Many thrills and high interest rates for own good. Muggers.
Much lead in petrol. Filth. Rule Britannia and child abuse.
Electronic tagging, Boss, ten pints and plenty rape. Queen Mum.
Channel Tunnel. You get here fast no problem to my country
my country my country welcome welcome welcome.

1989년, 영국을 번역하기

'... 그리고 많은 시들이, 아, 번역에 몰두하고 있다 ...'

우리나라에 오신 것을 환영합니다! 우리 이곳에는 에드위나 큐리와
선 신문이 있어요. 굉장히 재미가 있죠.
게다가 날씨는 2월에도 온화하게 되었어요
수선화 꽃도 피구요. (워즈워스가 있죠. 위 북쪽으로.)
셰익스피어나 오페라를 좋아한다면 우리는 암표시장도 있지요.
이백 파운드로 우리는 레미제라불을 이야기하지요,
윙크하듯이 고개를 끄덕이지요. 달걀은 먹지 마세요.
단속용 차량 바퀴 죔쇠, 개들, 부랑자도 있지요. 우리의 멋진
수도(首都) 관광도 놓치시면 안되죠. 그룹 퍼기,
다이아나 황태자비와 축구 광팬들이 있구요, 당신들은 진정으로
이곳에 있는 대지주를 좋아할 거예요. 게다가 내키기만 하면
우리는 깨부수고 때리는 것과 칼링 블랙 라벨 맥주에 대해 이야기할 수 있어요.
물은 마시지 마세요. 자랑스럽게도 우리는 지금
녹색당 총리가 있답니다. 당신네 총리는 어떤 색이죠? 쓰레기봉투들이 있죠.
당신들은 찰스 디킨스와 테리 우건 그리고 스코틀랜드에
대해 알거예요. 이 모든 것이 의심할 여지 없이 현금으로 진행되죠.
아일랜드에는 안 가요. 피시앤 칩스와 공직자 비밀 엄수법은
세계 최고죠. 자 이제 시작됩니다. 우리는
부동산 회사나 네이버스처럼 정말 재밌는 시간이 좋아요.
브룩사이드 채널도요. 우리는 네 채널이 있죠.
당신네 나라는 얼마나 많이 있나요? 지난밤에 열린 무도회들. 앤드류
로이브-웨버. 제프리 아쳐. 당신들이 즐길 수 있는 풍성한 문화가 있을 거예요.
또한 역사와 건축물들도 있구요. 상원의회. 런던 항만지구가 있어요.
우리를 위한 엄청난 스릴과 높은 금리가 있죠. 노상강도들도 있고요.
휘발유에는 납성분이 많죠. 쓰레기오물들도요. 애국가와 아동학대도요.
전자감지시스템, 보스 게임, 맥주집 입장료와 풍성한 강간이 있죠. 여왕
엄마도요.
해저 터널이 있고요. 문제없으니 이곳 우리나라로 빨리 오세요.
우리나라 우리나라 환영해요 환영해요 환영해요.

Valentine

Not a red rose or a satin heart.

I give you an onion.
It is a moon wrapped in brown paper.
It promises light
like the careful undressing of love.

Here.
It will blind you with tears
like a lover.
It will make your reflection
a wobbling photo of grief.

I am trying to be truthful.

Not a cute card or a kissogram.

I give you an onion.
Its fierce kiss will stay on your lips,
possessive and faithful
as we are,
for as long as we are.

Take it.
Its platinum loops shrink to a wedding-ring,
if you like.

Lethal.
Its scent will cling to your fingers,
cling to your knife.

발렌타인

빨간 장미나 공단으로 짠 하트는 아냐.

나는 네게 양파를 준다.
그것은 갈색 봉투에 싸인 달이지.
그것은 조심스럽게 벗겨지는 사랑처럼
빛을 약속하지.

그래
그것은 연인처럼
눈물로 너를 눈멀게 하지.
그것은 반사된 너의 모습을
떨리는 슬픈 사진이 되게 하지.

나는 진실 되려 해.

귀여운 카드나 키스 대행은 아니야.

나는 네게 양파를 준다.
그것의 격렬한 입맞춤은 너의 입술에 머물러
소유하려고, 충실하려고
바로 우리처럼
할 수 있는 한 오래.

가져가.
그 백금색 고리는 결혼반지처럼 작아지지
네가 원한다면 말이야.

치명적이지.
그 냄새는 네 손가락에 들러붙고
네 칼에 들러붙겠지.

Warming Her Pearls

for Judith Radstone

Next to my own skin, her pearls. My mistress
bids me wear them, warm them, until evening
when I'll brush her hair. At six, I place them
round her cool, white throat. All day I think of her,

resting in the Yellow Room, contemplating silk
or taffeta, which gown tonight? She fans herself
whilst I work willingly, my slow heat entering
each pearl. Slack on my neck, her rope.

She's beautiful. I dream about her
in my attic bed; picture her dancing
with tall men, puzzled by my faint, persistent scent
beneath her French perfume, her milky stones.

I dust her shoulders with a rabbit's foot,
watch the soft blush seep through her skin
like an indolent sigh. In her looking-glass
my red lips part as though I want to speak.

Full moon. Her carriage brings her home. I see
her every movement in my head.... Undressing,
taking off her jewels, her slim hand reaching
for the case, slipping naked into bed, the way

she always does.... And I lie here awake,
knowing the pearls are cooling even now
in the room where my mistress sleeps. All night
I feel their absence and I burn.

그녀의 진주 목걸이 데우기

쥬디스 래드스톤을 위해

바로 내 피부 위, 그녀의 진주 목걸이. 내가 걸쳐서
따뜻하게 하라고 내 애인이 말했지, 그녀의 머리를 빗겨주는
저녁까지. 여섯시면 나는 그녀의 차갑고 하얀 목 위에
그 목걸이를 걸어주지. 하루 종일 그녀를 생각해,

노란 방에서 쉬며 실크 옷을 입을까 아니면 태피터 옷을 입을까,
어떤 가운을 입을까 고심하는 그녀를, 그녀는 내가 기꺼이 일하는 동안
부채질을 하네, 그래 내 몸의 열기가 천천히 진주 방울방울
스며드네. 내 목 위에 느즈러진 그녀의 밧줄.

아름다운 그녀. 나 다락방의
침대에 누워 그녀를 꿈꾸네, 그녀의 프랑스 향수아래
옅지만 오래가는 내 향기에 놀란, 키 큰 남자와 춤추는
그녀를 마음에 그리네, 그녀의 우유 빛 보석.

나는 토끼발 털이개로 그녀의 어깨를 털어낸다,
나른한 숨처럼 그녀의 피부로 새어나오는 흐릿한
홍조를 지켜본다. 그녀의 거울 속에서
나의 입술은 벌어진다, 마치 할 말이 있다는 듯이.

보름달, 그녀의 마차가 그녀를 집으로 데려오네. 나는 내 머리 속에서
그녀의 모든 움직임을 보고 있네.... 옷을 벗고, 보석들을 풀어 놓고,
가느다란 손이 보석 상자에 닿는 것을, 옷 벗은 몸을 침대 속으로
미끄러져 누이는 것을, 그녀가 항상

그러하듯이.... 나 여기 깨어 누워 있네
그 진주들은 지금 내 애인이 잠든 방안에서
차가워지고 있다고 생각하면서, 밤새
나 그것들이 내 목 위에 없음을 느끼며, 불타오르네.

Edwin Arlington Robinson (1869-1935)

On December 22, 1869, Edwin Arlington Robinson was born in Head Tide, Maine (the same year as W. B. Yeats). His family moved to Gardiner, Maine, in 1870, which renamed "Tilbury Town," became the backdrop for many of Robinson's poems. Robinson described his childhood as stark and unhappy; he once wrote in a letter to Amy Lowell that he remembered wondering why he had been born at the age of six. After high school, Robinson spent two years studying at Harvard University as a special student and his first poems were published in the *Harvard Advocate*.

Robinson privately printed and released his first volume of poetry, *The Torrent and the Night Before*, in 1896 at his own expense; this collection was extensively revised and published in 1897 as *The Children of the Night*. Unable to make a living by writing, he got a job as an inspector for the New York City subway system. In 1902 he published *Captain Craig and Other Poems*. This work received little attention until President Theodore Roosevelt wrote a magazine article praising it and Robinson. Roosevelt also offered Robinson a sinecure in a U.S. Customs House, a job he held from 1905 to 1910. Robinson dedicated his next work, *The Town Down the River* (1910), to Roosevelt. Robinson's first major success was *The Man Against the Sky* (1916). He also composed a trilogy based on Arthurian legends: *Merlin* (1917), *Lancelot* (1920), and *Tristram* (1927), which won a Pulitzer Prize in 1928. Robinson was also awarded a Pulitzer Prize for his *Collected Poems* (1921) in 1922 and *The Man Who Died Twice* (1924) in 1925.

Some of Robinson's poetry present characters and social environments of the kind found in the realistic novels of the nineteenth century, although never in its poetry. The mingling of tenderness and irony in his poems was also unusual at a time when most poetry still maintained the undeviating seriousness that was conventional in the nineteenth century.

For the last twenty-five years of his life, Robinson spent his summers at the MacDowell Colony of artists and musicians in Peterborough, New Hampshire. Robinson never married and led a notoriously solitary lifestyle. He died in New York City on April 6, 1935.

Credo

I cannot find my way: there is no star
In all the shrouded heavens anywhere;
And there is not a whisper in the air
Of any living voice but one so far
That I can hear it only as a bar
Of lost, imperial music, played when fair
And angel fingers wove, and unaware,
Dead leaves to garlands where no roses are.

No, there is not a glimmer, nor a call,
For one that welcomes, welcomes when he fears,
The black and awful chaos of the night;
For through it all—above, beyond it all—
I know the far sent message of the years,
I feel the coming glory of the light.

신조

길을 찾을 수 없다. 수의를 입은
하늘에는 어디에도 별이 없다.
대기에는 살아있는 목소리의
속삭임은 없고 다만 먼 소리가 있어
잃어버린 장엄한 음악의 소절로만 들려온다.
그것은 아름다운 천사의 손가락이 장미 없는 화환에
남 몰래 죽은 잎들을 엮을 때에 연주되었던 것이다.

밤의 검고 무서운 혼돈을 맞아들이는 자에게는,
두려운 마음일 때 맞아들이는 자에게는
깜박이는 빛도 없고 부르는 소리도 없지만,
혼돈을 통해—그 위와 그 너머로부터—
세월의 아득한 송신이 있고
빛의 영광이 다가옴을 나는 느낀다.

The House on the Hill

They are all gone away,
    The house is shut and still,
There is nothing more to say.

Through broken walls and gray
    The winds blow bleak and shrill:
They are all gone away.

Nor is there one today
    To speak them good or ill:
There is nothing more to say.

Why is it then we stray
    Around the sunken sill?
They are all gone away.

And our poor fancy-play
    For them is wasted skill:
There is nothing more to say.

There is ruin and decay
    In the House on the Hill
They are all gone away,
There is nothing more to say.

언덕 위의 집

그들이 모두 가 버려
　　그 집은 닫힌 채 고요하고
더 이상 아무 할 말이 없다.

무너진 잿빛 벽들 사이로
　　바람이 황량하고 날카롭게 부는데,
그들은 모두 가 버렸다.

이제 그들을 칭찬하거나 험담할
　　사람 아무도 없다.
더 이상 아무 할 말이 없다.

그런데 우리가 그 주저앉은 문지방
　　주위를 서성임은 왠가?
그들은 모두 가 버렸는데.

또한 그들에 대한 우리의 서툰
　　상상의 유희는 헛된 재주일 뿐,
더 이상 아무 할 말이 없다.

붕괴와 쇠락이 있다,
　　언덕 위의 집에.
그들은 모두 가 버렸고,
더 이상 아무 할 말이 없다.

Miniver Cheevy

Miniver Cheevy, child of scorn,
  Grew lean while he assailed the seasons;
He wept that he was ever born,
  And he had reasons.

Miniver loved the days of old
  When swords were bright and steeds were prancing;
The vision of a warrior bold
  Would set him dancing.

Miniver sighed for what was not,
  And dreamed, and rested from his labors;
He dreamed of Thebes and Camelot,
  And Priam's neighbors.

Miniver mourned the ripe renown
  That made so many a name so fragrant;
He mourned Romance, now on the town,
  And Art, a vagrant.

Miniver loved the Medici,
  Albeit he had never seen one;
He would have sinned incessantly
  Could he have been one.

Miniver cursed the commonplace
  And eyed a khaki suit with loathing;
He missed the mediæval grace
  Of iron clothing.

미니버 취비

조롱거리 아이 미니버 치비는
　　세월을 맹공하느라 여위었다.
그는 태어난 것에 대해 울었는데,
　　그에겐 그럴 이유가 있었다.

미니버는 옛날을 사랑했다,
　　검들이 빛나고 말들이 뒷발로 뛰어오르던 그때를.
대담한 무사의 환상이
　　그를 춤추게 하기도 했다.

미니버는 없는 것이 그리워 한숨쉬었고,
　　꿈을 꾸었고, 일한 뒤엔 쉬었다.
그는 테베와 카멜롯에 대해,
　　프라아모스의 이웃들에 대해 꿈꾸었다.

미니버는 수많은 이름들을 그토록 향기롭게 한
　　무르익은 고명을 애도했다.
그는 애도했다, 이제 생계보조대상이 된 로망스와
　　부랑자가 된 예술을.

미니버는 메디치가 사람들을 사랑했다,
　　비록 한 사람도 본 적은 없지만.
만약 메디치가 사람이 될 수만 있다면
　　쉬지 않고 죄를 지으려고도 했을 것이다.

미니버는 평범한 것을 저주했고
　　카키색 양복을 혐오하면서 쳐다보았다.
그는 그리워했다,
　　철제 갑옷의 중세풍 우아함을.

미니버는 그가 얻으려한 황금을 경멸했지만,
　　그것이 없어 심히 곤욕을 치렀다.
그는 생각하고, 생각하고, 생각하고,
　　또 생각했다, 그것에 대해.

너무 늦게 태어난 미니버 치비는,
　　머리를 긁으면서 계속 생각했다.
미니버는 기침을 하고, 그것을 운명이라고 부르고는,
　　계속 술을 마셨다.

Miniver scorned the gold he sought,
　But sore annoyed was he without it;
Miniver thought, and thought, and thought,
　And thought about it.

Miniver Cheevy, born too late,
　Scratched his head and kept on thinking;
Miniver coughed, and called it fate,
　And kept on drinking.

Oh for a Poet – For a Beacon Bright

OH for a poet — for a beacon bright
To rift this changless glimmer of dead gray;
To spirit back the Muses, long astray,
And flush Parnassus with a newer light;
To put these little sonnet-men to flight
Who fashion, in a shrewd mechanic way,
Songs without souls, that flicker for a day,
To vanish in irrevocable night.

What does it mean, this barren age of ours?
Here are the men, the women, and the flowers,
The seasons, and the sunset, as before.
What does it mean? Shall there not one arise
To wrench one banner from the western skies,
And mark it with his name forevermore?

빛나는 횃불을 위하여

아 성인이—빛나는 횃불이 있었으면,
이 변함없는 죽은 회색의 어둠을 깨끗이 찢어 버릴.
오래 방황하던 시신들을 데불고 와서
새 빛으로 파나서스 산을 붉게 물들여 놓았으면.
그리하여, 약은 기계적 방법으로 하루를 반짝이다
영원한 밤으로 사라지는
얼 없는 노래들을 만들어 내는
시시한 친구들을 멀리 쫓아 버렸으면.

도대체 무엇인가, 메마른 이 시대는?
남자와 여자와 꽃이 있고
계절 일몰도 여전히 있다.
도대체 무엇인가? 서녘 하늘로부터
한 기치 뽑아내어 영원히 제 이름 아로새길
한 사람 없을 것인가?

Reuben Bright

Because he was a butcher and thereby
Did earn an honest living (and did right),
I would not have you think that Reuben Bright
Was any more a brute than you or I;
For when they told him that his wife must die,
He stared at them, and shook with grief and fright,
And cried like a great baby half that night,
And made the women cry to see him cry.

And after she was dead, and he had paid
The singers and the sexton and the rest,
He packed a lot of things that she had made
Most mournfully away in an old chest
Of hers, and put some chopped-up cedar boughs
In with them, and tore down the slaughter-house.

루벤 브라이트

푸줏간을 벌여놓고
먹고 사는 자라 하여
루벤 브라이트가 당신이나 나보다
못한 사람이라고는 생각하지 말라.
아내가 죽게 됐다고 사람들이 말했을 때
그는 그들을 빤히 쳐다보더니, 슬픔과 두려움에 몸을 떨면서,
그날밤 반을 어린애처럼 울며 새웠다.
그가 우는 모습에 여인들도 따라 울었다.

아내가 죽은 후에, 노래해 준 이들과
묘를 파 준 사람과 나머지 사람들에게 사례한 후
아내가 만든 많은 물건을
그녀의 낡은 궤 속에 아주 슬프게
쳐넣고, 삼나무 가지도 몇 개 잘라
함께 넣고, 도살장을 허물었다.

Richard Cory

Whenever Richard Cory went down town,
We people on the pavement looked at him:
He was a gentleman from sole to crown,
Clean favored, and imperially slim.

And he was always quietly arrayed,
And he was always human when he talked;
But still he fluttered pulses when he said,
'Good-morning,' and he glittered when he walked.

And he was rich - yes, richer than a king -
And admirably schooled in every grace:
In fine, we thought that he was everything
To make us wish that we were in his place.

So on we worked, and waited for the light,
And went without the meat, and cursed the bread;
And Richard Cory, one calm summer night,
Went home and put a bullet through his head.

리차드 코리

리차드 코리가 시내에 나가면,
우리들 포도 위의 사람들은 그를 쳐다보았다.
그는 발끝에서 머리까지 신사였다,
말쑥한 용모에 황제처럼 날씬했다.

그리고 그는 항상 점잖게 옷차림을 하고,
이야길 할 땐 언제나 인간미가 있었다.
그러나 그가 "안녕하십니까" 할 때엔
여전히 사람들을 흥분시켰고, 걸어갈 땐 번쩍번쩍 빛났다.

그리고 그는 부자였다—그렇다, 왕보다 부자였다,
그리고 감탄할만큼 모든 면에서 훌륭한 교육을 받았었다.
요컨대, 우리는 생각했다, 그는 어느 모로나
우리에게 그의 입장을 부러워하게 하는 사람이라고.

그리하여 우리는 일을 계속하며, 광명을 기다렸다.
그리고, 고기도 없이 지냈고 빵을 저주했다.
그런데 리차드 코리는 어느 고요한 여름 밤에
집에 돌아가 제 머리에 총을 쏘았다.

Robert Frost (1874-1963)

Robert Frost was born on March 26, 1874, in San Francisco, where his father, William Prescott Frost Jr., and his mother, Isabelle Moodie, had moved from Pennsylvania shortly after marrying. After the death of his father from tuberculosis when Frost was eleven years old, he moved with his mother and sister, Jeanie, who was two years younger, to Lawrence, Massachusetts. He became interested in reading and writing poetry during his high school years in Lawrence, enrolled at Dartmouth College in Hanover, New Hampshire, in 1892, and later at Harvard University in Boston, though he never earned a formal college degree.

In 1895, Frost married Elinor Miriam White, whom he'd shared valedictorian honors with in high school and who was a major inspiration for his poetry until her death in 1938. The couple moved to England in 1912, after they tried and failed at farming in New Hampshire. It was abroad that Frost met and was influenced by such contemporary British poets as Edward Thomas, Rupert Brooke, and Robert Graves. While in England, Frost also established a friendship with the poet Ezra Pound, who helped to promote and publish his work.

Though his work is principally associated with the life and landscape of New England — and though he was a poet of traditional verse forms and metrics who remained steadfastly aloof from the poetic movements and fashions of his time — Frost is anything but merely a regional poet. The author of searching and often dark meditations on universal themes, he is a quintessentially modern poet in his adherence to language as it is actually spoken, in the psychological complexity of his portraits, and in the degree to which his work is infused with layers of ambiguity and irony.

In a 1970 review of *The Poetry of Robert Frost*, the poet Daniel Hoffman describes Frost's early work as "the Puritan ethic turned astonishingly lyrical and enabled to say out loud the sources of its own delight in the world," and comments on Frost's career as the "American Bard": "He became a national celebrity, our nearly official poet laureate, and a great performer in the tradition of that earlier master of the literary vernacular, Mark Twain."

About Frost, President John F. Kennedy, at whose inauguration the poet delivered a poem, said, "He has bequeathed his nation a body of imperishable verse from which Americans will forever gain joy and understanding."

Robert Frost lived and taught for many years in Massachusetts and Vermont, and died in Boston on January 29, 1963.

Birches

When I see birches bend to left and right
Across the lines of straighter darker trees,
I like to think some boy's been swinging them.
But swinging doesn't bend them down to stay.
Ice-storms do that. Often you must have seen them
Loaded with ice a sunny winter morning
After a rain. They click upon themselves
As the breeze rises, and turn many-coloured
As the stir cracks and crazes their enamel.
Soon the sun's warmth makes them shed crystal shells
Shattering and avalanching on the snow-crust
Such heaps of broken glass to sweep away
You'd think the inner dome of heaven had fallen.
They are dragged to the withered bracken by the load,
And they seem not to break; though once they are bowed
So low for long, they never right themselves:
You may see their trunks arching in the woods
Years afterwards, trailing their leaves on the ground,
Like girls on hands and knees that throw their hair
Before them over their heads to dry in the sun.
But I was going to say when Truth broke in
With all her matter-of-fact about the ice-storm,
I should prefer to have some boy bend them
As he went out and in to fetch the cows-
Some boy too far from town to learn baseball,
Whose only play was what he found himself,
Summer or winter, and could play alone.
One by one he subdued his father's trees
By riding them down over and over again
Until he took the stiffness out of them,

자작나무들

줄지어 곧게 뻗은 검은 나무들 좌우로
자작나무들이 이리저리 휘어지는 걸 볼 때
나는 어떤 아이가 거기 매달려 그넬 타고 있다고 생각하게 된다.
그러나 매달리는 것으론 얼음덩이만큼 그걸 구부려
꼼짝 못하게 할 수 없다. 비 개고 햇빛 밝은
겨울 날 아침, 자작나무에 얼음이 가득 실려 있는 걸
자주 보았으리라. 바람이 일어 그것이 탁탁 소리 내며,
흔들려 거죽에 금이 가고 갈라지며 색색으로 변한다.
곧 태양의 온기 받으면 수정 같은 외피가 산산이 부서져
눈 덮인 땅 위에 사태가 난다—
이런 깨어진 유리더미를 휩쓸어 내리느라고
하늘의 내면 둥근 천정이 내려앉은 거라고 생각하리라.
가지가 무게 때문에 끌려서 시든 고사리 숲까지 닿지만
꺾일 것 같진 않다. 한 번 휘어져내려
오래 되면 다시 곧게 서질 않지만.
몇 년 뒤에 그 가지들이 잎을 땅에 끌며
숲 속에 궁문을 이루는 것을 보게 된다, 마치 소녀들이 손 지고 무릎 꿇고 고개를 수그리고
머리를 햇볕에 말리려고 앞으로 내려뜨린 것과 같이.
그러나 그 얼음덩이에 관한 '사실'을
진리로 깨달았을 때에도 나는 이렇게 말하고 싶었다.
즉, 어떤 소년이 소를 끌고 드나들 때에
그 애가 나무를 구부려 놓았다고 생각하고 싶다.—
그 아이는 도시에서 멀리 살기 때문에 야구를 모른다.
놀이란 오직 제가 생각해낸 것이고,
여름 겨울 없이 혼자서 놀 뿐.
그 아이는 하나 하나 아버지의 나무를 정복했다,
거기 올라 타고 또 올라 타서
나무를 시들부들하게 만들고야 말았다.

And not one but hung limp, not one was left
For him to conquer. He learned all there was
To learn about not launching out too soon
And so not carrying the tree away
Clear to the ground. He always kept his poise
To the top branches, climbing carefully
With the same pains you use to fill a cup
Up to the brim, and even above the brim.
Then he flung outward, feet first, with a swish,
Kicking his way down through the air to the ground.
So was I once myself a swinger of birches.
And so I dream of going back to be.
It's when I'm weary of considerations,
And life is too much like a pathless wood
Where your face burns and tickles with the cobwebs
Broken across it, and one eye is weeping
From a twig's having lashed across it open.
I'd like to get away from earth awhile
And then come back to it and begin over.
May no fate willfully misunderstand me
And half grant what I wish and snatch me away
Not to return. Earth's the right place for love:
I don't know where it's likely to go better.
I'd like to go by climbing a birch tree
And climb black branches up a snow-white trunk
Toward heaven, till the tree could bear no more,
But dipped its top and set me down again.
That would be good both going and coming back.
One could do worse than be a swinger of birches.

축 처진 병신 가시 밖엔 더 정복할 가지라곤
하나도 안 남았다. 그 아이는 알게 되었다,
너무 빨리 착수해서 나무를
지상에서 아주 말끔히 쓸어버려선
안 되겠다는 것을. 그 아이는 늘 가지 꼭대기까지
몸의 균형을 취하며 조심껏 올라갔다,
물 잔을 찰랑찰랑, 아니 소복히 될 때까지
잔을 채울 때 만큼이나 그렇게 힘들여서.
그리고는 발부터 먼저 몸을 던져
휙하고 하늘을 날아 지상으로 뛰어내린다.
나 자신도 한 때 자작나무에 매달릴 때 그랬다.
그리고 그렇게 그때로 돌아가기를 꿈꾼다.
내가 생각에 시달리고, 인생이
말하자면 길 없는 숲 속 같아,
흩어진 거미줄에 걸려 얼굴은 화끈화끈 군시럽고
한쪽 눈은 뜬 채 작은 가지에 얻어맞아
눈물이 나는 그런 때.
나는 잠시 이 세상에서 떠났다가
다시 돌아와서 되 시작했으면 싶다,
제발 운명이 심술궂게 나를 곡해하여
내 소원을 전연 용납 않고 나를 채가서
다시 돌아오지 못하게 하지 않기를.
지상은 당연히 사랑할 만한 곳이다.
어디로 가면 더 나을지 난 모른다.
난 자작나루를 타고 올라갔으면 싶다.
검은 가지를 올라
하늘 향하여 눈처럼 흰 줄기까지 이르고 싶다, 나무가 무게에 겨워
그 끝을 땅에 대고, 나를 도로 내려 놀 때까지.
가는 것 돌아오는 것 다 좋으리라.
사람은 자작나무에 그네 타는 것보다 더 나쁜 일을 할 수도 있으리라.

Come In

As I came to the edge of the woods,
Thrush music — hark!
Now if it was dusk outside,
Inside it was dark.

Too dark in the woods for a bird
By sleight of wing
To better its perch for the night,
Though it still could sing.

The last of the light of the sun
That had died in the west
Still lived for one song more
In a thrush's breast.

Far in the pillared dark
Thrush music went —
Almost like a call to come in
To the dark and lament.

But no, I was out for stars;
I would not come in.
I meant not even if asked;
And I hadn't been.

들어오라

내가 숲 가에 갔을 때,
들어라 — 지빠귀새의 노래 소리!
그 때 밖은 황혼이지만
내부는 어두웠다.

숲 속이 너무 어두워
새는 날개의 재간으로도
잠자리를 옮길 순 없었다,
아직 노랠 부를 순 있었지만.

서쪽에 진
태양의 마지막 광선이
아직 지빠귀새의 가슴에 살아 있었다,
한 마디 노래를 더 부르기 위하여.

기둥진 어둠 속 깊이
지빠귀새의 노래 소리 울렸다—
어둠 속에 들어와
서러워하라는 듯이.

그러나, 아니다, 나는 별을 보러 나왔었다
나는 들어가지 않겠다.
오라 한들 들어갈 생각이 없었다.
아니, 들어오란 말 들은 일도 없었다.

Mending Wall

Something there is that doesn't love a wall,
That sends the frozen-ground-swell under it,
And spills the upper boulders in the sun;
And makes gaps even two can pass abreast.
The work of hunters is another thing:
I have come after them and made repair
Where they have left not one stone on a stone,
But they would have the rabbit out of hiding,
To please the yelping dogs. The gaps I mean,
No one has seen them made or heard them made,
But at spring mending-time we find them there.
I let my neighbour know beyond the hill;
And on a day we meet to walk the line
And set the wall between us once again.
We keep the wall between us as we go.
To each the boulders that have fallen to each.
And some are loaves and some so nearly balls
We have to use a spell to make them balance:
"Stay where you are until our backs are turned!"
We wear our fingers rough with handling them.
Oh, just another kind of out-door game,
One on a side. It comes to little more:
There where it is we do not need the wall:
He is all pine and I am apple orchard.
My apple trees will never get across
And eat the cones under his pines, I tell him.
He only says, "Good fences make good neighbours."
Spring is the mischief in me, and I wonder
If I could put a notion in his head:

담장 고치기

담장을 싫어하는 무엇이 있어
그 아래에서 서릿발을 솟게 하여
위쪽의 돌덩이들을 햇빛 속에 쏟고
두 사람이 나란히 지나갈 만한 틈을 만든다.
사냥꾼들이 한 짓은 별개다.
그들 뒤에 내가 와서 그들이
완전히 헤쳐 놓은 것을 고쳤다.
그래도 그들은 숨어있는 토끼들을 몰아내어
짖어대는 개들을 즐겁게 해주곤 했다. 내가 말하는 틈이란,
그것이 생기는 것을 본 사람도 들은 사람도 없는데
봄철 수리 때 보면 거기에 있었다.
나는 언덕 너머 이웃 사람에게 알려
하루 날 잡아 경계선을 따라 걸으며
우리 사이에 다시 담장을 쌓는다.
우리는 담장을 사이에 두고 걸어간다.
각자 자기 쪽에 떨어진 돌들을 맡는다.
어떤 것들은 빵떡 같고 어떤 것들은 공 같아서
그것들을 균형있게 쌓아 올리는 데엔 주문을 외워야 한다,
"우리가 돌아설 때까지 그대로 있으렴."
돌을 만지느라 손이 거칠어진다.
한 편이 한 사람씩인 일종의
야외 경기일 뿐 그 이상은 아니다.
그 자리에 담장은 필요 없다.
그의 것은 솔밭이고 나의 것은 사과밭인데
나는 내 사과나무가 저쪽으로 건너가서
떨어진 솔방울을 먹을 리가 없다고 그에게 말한다.
그는 "좋은 울타리가 좋은 이웃을 만들지요"라고 말할 뿐이다.
봄이 나를 짓궂게 하여 혹시 그의 머리에
어떤 생각을 넣을 수 있을까 싶어 말했다,

"Why do they make good neighbours? Isn't it
Where there are cows? But here there are no cows.
Before I built a wall I'd ask to know
What I was walling in or walling out,
And to whom I was like to give offence.
Something there is that doesn't love a wall,
That wants it down." I could say "Elves" to him,
But it's not elves exactly, and I'd rather
He said it for himself. I see him there
Bringing a stone grasped firmly by the top
In each hand, like an old-stone savage armed.
He moves in darkness as it seems to me,
Not of woods only and the shade of trees.
He will not go behind his father's saying,
And he likes having thought of it so well
He says again, "Good fences make good neighbours."

"어째서 그렇지요? 그것은
소 있는 곳에나 그런 것 아닐까요? 여기는 소가 없는데.
담장을 쌓기 전에 물어보고 싶었지요
내가 무엇을 이쪽 저쪽으로 갈라 막는 건지요,
내가 누구 비위를 거슬러 이러는지요
담장을 좋아하지 않는 무언가가 있어
허물고 싶어하는 건지요." "요정"이라고 그에게 말하고 싶었지만
엄밀하게 말하면 요정은 아니고, 차라리
그가 스스로 말했으면 한다. 저기 그가
무장한 구석기 시대 야만인처럼 한 손에 한 개씩
돌머리를 단단히 쥐고 들고 오는 것이 보인다.
내게는 그가 어둠 속에서 움직이는 것 같다.
숲이나 나무 그늘의 어둠만이 아닌.
그는 그의 아버지가 한 말을 따지지 않으려 한다.
그게 마침 그렇게 잘 생각났던 것이 좋아서
그는 다시 말한다, "좋은 울타리가 좋은 이웃을 만들지요."

The Road not Taken

Two roads diverged in a yellow wood,
And sorry I could not travel both
And be one traveler, long I stood
And looked down one as far as I could
To where it bent in the undergrowth;

Then took the other, as just as fair,
And having perhaps the better claim
Because it was grassy and wanted wear,
Though as for that the passing there
Had worn them really about the same,

And both that morning equally lay
In leaves no step had trodden black.
Oh, I kept the first for another day!
Yet knowing how way leads on to way
I doubted if I should ever come back.

I shall be telling this with a sigh
Somewhere ages and ages hence:
Two roads diverged in a wood, and I,
I took the one less traveled by,
And that has made all the difference.

가지 않은 길

두 길이 누런 숲 속에서 갈라져 있었다.
유감이지만 나는 두 길을 다 갈 수 없는
한 사람의 여행자였다. 오랫동안 서서
한쪽 길이 덤불 속으로 구부러져 들어간 쪽을
멀리 시선이 닿는 한 바라다보았다.

그리곤 다른 쪽 길을 택했다. 역시 아름다운,
그럴만한 당연한 이유가 있었다,
거기에는 풀이 많고 아직 밟혀 있지 않았기에.
사실 그 점으로 말하면 두 길이
거의 같은 정도로 통행인에게 밟혀져 있었고,

또한 그날 아침은 두 길이 모두
아무에게도 밟혀 더럽혀지지 않은 낙엽 속에 묻혀 있었다.
아, 나는 한 쪽 길은 후일에 가기로 했다!
그러나 길은 길로 나아가는 것임을 알기에
내가 과연 돌아올 것인지 의심했다.

나는 이 말을 한숨지며 말하리라,
지금부터 여러 해 여러 해 뒤 어딘가에서.
숲 속에 두 길이 갈라져 있었는데, 나는 —
나는 덜 다닌 길을 택했었고,
그런데 그것이 아주 큰 차이를 가져왔다고.

Stopping by Woods on a Snowy Evening

Whose woods these are I think I know.
His house is in the village, though;
He will not see me stopping here
To watch his woods fill up with snow.

My little horse must think it queer
To stop without a farmhouse near
Between the woods and frozen lake
The darkest evening of the year.

He gives his harness bells a shake
To ask if there is some mistake.
The only other sound's the sweep
Of easy wind and downy flake.

The woods are lovely, dark and deep,
But I have promises to keep,
And miles to go before I sleep,
And miles to go before I sleep.

눈 오는 저녁 숲 가에 서서

이것이 누구네 숲인지 알 것 같다.
그의 집이 마을에 있긴 하지만,
그는 내가 여기 서서 그의 숲에
눈이 쌓이는 것을 바라보는 것이 보이지 않으리라.

나의 작은 말은 이상하게 생각하리라,
숲과 언 호수 사이
근처에 농가도 없는 곳에 멈춘 것을,
일년 중 가장 어두운 저녁에.

말은 무슨 착오라도 있느냐고 묻는 듯이
마구에 달린 방울을 흔든다.
달리 들리는 소리라곤 오직
솜털 같은 눈송이를 휩쓰는 거리낌 없는 바람 소리 뿐.

숲은 아름답고, 어둡고 깊다.
그러나 나는 약속한 일을 지켜야겠고,
자기 전에 몇 마일을 가야겠다,
자기 전에 몇 마일을 가야겠다.

Tree at My Window

Tree at my window, window tree,
My sash is lowered when night comes on;
But let there never be curtain drawn
Between you and me.

Vague dream head lifted out of the ground,
And thing next most diffuse to cloud,
Not all your light tongues talking aloud
Could be profound.

But tree, I have seen you taken and tossed,
And if you have seen me when I slept,
You have seen me when I was taken and swept
And all but lost.

That day she put our heads together,
Fate had her imagination about her,
Your head so much concerned with outer,
Mine with inner, weather.

창 가의 나무

창 가의 나무, 창 나무야,
밤이 오면 나는 들창문을 내린다,
그러나 커튼은 치지 말자,
너와 나 사이엔.

희미하게 꿈꾸는 머리를 땅으로부터 치켜든,
구름 다음으론 가장 산만한 것이여,
큰 소리로 말하는 너의 경쾌한 지껄임이
모두 심각할 리가 없다.

그러나 나는 네가 정신이 빼겨 나가떨어진 것을 본 일이 있다,
그리고, 만일 네가 나의 잠잘 때 모습을 본 일이 있다면
너는 내가 무엇에 사로잡혀 쏠려 있는 것을 보았으리라,
거의 정신이 팔린 것을.

그날 운명은 우리 둘의 머리를 맞대놓고,
상상에 골몰했다,
너의 머리는 온통 바깥 날씨에 쏠리고,
내 머리는 심중의, 날씨에 쏠려 있었다.

Wallace Stevens (1879-1955)

Wallace Stevens was born in Reading, Pennsylvania, on October 2, 1879. He attended Harvard University as an undergraduate from 1897 to 1900. He planned to travel to Paris as a writer, but after a working briefly as a reporter for the *New York Herald Times*, he decided to study law. He graduated with a degree from New York Law School in 1903 and was admitted to the U.S. Bar in 1904. He practiced law in New York City until 1916. Though he had serious determination to become a successful lawyer, Stevens had several friends among the New York writers and painters in Greenwich Village, including the poets William Carlos Williams, Marianne Moore, and E. E. Cummings.

In 1914, under the pseudonym "Peter Parasol," he sent a group of poems under the title "Phases" to Harriet Monroe for a war poem competition for *Poetry* magazine. Stevens did not win the prize, but was published by Monroe in November of that year. Stevens moved to Connecticut in 1916, having found employment at the Hartford Accident and Indemnity Co., of which he became vice president in 1934.

He had begun to establish an identity for himself outside the world of law and business, however, and his first book of poems, *Harmonium*, published in 1923, exhibited the influence of both the English Romantics and the French symbolists, an inclination to aesthetic philosophy, and a wholly original style and sensibility: exotic, whimsical, infused with the light and color of an Impressionist painting. The general theme of all Stevens' later poetry is the difference between reality as it is in itself and as it is perceived imaginatively. But the illustrations of this theme vary enormously from poem to poem, as does the balance of Stevens' allegiance between reality and imagination. The verve of Stevens' meditation tends to celebrate the dynamism of the human mind, our capacity of absorbed attention and continuing interest despite the poverty of our reality or experience. More than any other modern poet, Stevens was concerned with the transformative power of the imagination.

Though now considered one of the major American poets of the century, he did not receive widespread recognition until the publication of his *Collected Poems*, just a year before his death. His major works include *Ideas of Order* (1935), *The Man With the Blue Guitar* (1937), *Notes Towards a Supreme Fiction* (1942), and a collection of essays on poetry, *The Necessary Angel* (1951).

Stevens died in Hartford on August 2, 1955.

Anecdote of the Jar

I placed a jar in Tennessee,
And round it was, upon a hill.
It made the slovenly wilderness
Surround that hill.

The wilderness rose up to it,
And sprawled around, no longer wild.
The jar was round upon the ground
And tall and of a port in air.

It took dominion everywhere.
The jar was gray and bare.
It did not give of bird or bush,
Like nothing else in Tennessee.

항아리의 일화

나는 항아리 하나를 테네시주에 놓았다,
한 산 위에서 그것은 둥굴었다,
그것은 지저분한 황무지로
그 산을 에워싸게 만들었다.

황무지는 그것에까지 올라와
주변에 볼품없이 퍼졌으나 황폐는 끝났다.
항아리는 땅 위에서 둥글고
키가 크고 외관상 하나의 자태였다.

그것은 도처를 지배했다.
항아리는 회색이고 텅 비어있다.
그것은 새나 숲의 기색도 없고
테네시주의 다른 어떤 것과 달랐다.

The Emperor of Ice-Cream

Call the roller of big cigars,
The muscular one, and bid him whip
In kitchen cups concupiscent curds.
Let the wenches dawdle in such dress
As they are used to wear, and let the boys
Bring flowers in last month's newspapers.
Let be be finale of seem.
The only emperor is the emperor of ice-cream.

Take from the dresser of deal.
Lacking the three glass knobs, that sheet
On which she embroidered fantails once
And spread it so as to cover her face.
If her horny feet protrude, they come
To show how cold she is, and dumb.
Let the lamp affix its beam.
The only emperor is the emperor of ice-cream.

아이스크림 황제

큰 여송연 마는 사람을 불러라,
근육이 씩씩한 자를, 그리하여 그에게 일러
부엌의 컵에 식욕 돋구는 응유를 거품 일게 하라.
하녀들에게 보통 때 옷을 입고
빈둥거리게 하라, 그리고 소년들에게는
지난 달 신문지에 꽃을 싸 가지고 오게 하라.
실재를 현상의 궁극이 되게 하라.
유일한 황제는 아이스크림 황제이다.

유리 손잡이가 세 개 떨어진,
송판 장롱에서 그녀가 전에 공작 비둘기를 수 놓은
시트를 끄집어 내서
그 시트를 펼쳐 그녀의 얼굴을 덮어라.
만일 그녀의 굳은 발이 삐져 나온다면,
그녀가 싸늘하고, 말이 끊어졌음을 보여 줄 것이다.
램프로 하여금 불빛을 비치게 하라.
유일한 황제는 아이스크림 황제이다.

Of Modern Poetry

The poem of the mind in the act of finding
What will suffice. It has not always had
To find: the scene was set; it repeated what
Was in the script.
Then the theatre was changed
To something else. Its past was a souvenir.

It has to be living, to learn the speech of the place.
It has to face the men of the time and to meet
The women of the time. It has to think about war
And it has to find what will suffice. It has
To construct a new stage. It has to be on that stage,
And, like an insatiable actor, slowly and
With meditation, speak words that in the ear,
In the delicatest ear of the mind, repeat,
Exactly, that which it wants to hear, at the sound
Of which, an invisible audience listens,
Not to the play, but to itself, expressed
In an emotion as of two people, as of two
Emotions becoming one. The actor is
A metaphysician in the dark, twanging
An instrument, twanging a wiry string that gives
Sounds passing through sudden rightnesses, wholly
Containing the mind, below which it cannot descend,
Beyond which it has no will to rise.
It must
Be the finding of a satisfaction, and may
Be of a man skating, a woman dancing, a woman
Combing. The poem of the act of the mind.

현대시에 대하여

흡족한 것을 찾고자하는 연기에서
그 마음의 시. 그것은 반드시 찾아야
하는 것은 아니었다. 무대는 설정돼 있었고
대본에 있는 것을 되풀이 했다.
그 때 극장이 다른 것으로 바뀌었다,
그 과거는 하나의 기념품이었다.

시는 살아나가야 하고, 그 고장의 대사를 배워야 한다.
그 시대의 남자들과 대면해야 하고, 그 시대의
여자들과도, 전쟁에 대하여 생각해야하고
흡족한 것을 찾아야 한다. 새 무대를
만들어야 한다. 시는 그 무대 위에 올려져
끝내 만족을 모르는 배우처럼 천천히 그리고
명상하면서 대사를 말해야 한다. 그 말은
귀 속에서, 미묘한 마음의 귀에서, 정확히
그 귀가 듣고 싶은 것을 되풀이 해야 한다, 그음을 듣고서
눈에 안 보이는 청중이 귀 기울인다,
극에 대해서가 아니라, 마치
두 삶의 감정이 하나가 된 듯이 둘이 합쳐진
하나의 감정으로 표현된 그 말 자체에 귀 기울인다.
배우는 어둠 속의 형이상학자이다, 쾅쾅
악기를 울려대고, 쾅쾅 쇠줄을 뜯어댄다,
그 울림이 돌연한 올바름 속을 지나는 소리되어
완전히 마음을 내포하고, 시는 그 올바름 밑으로
내려갈 수도 없고 그 위로 올라가려 하지 않는다.
시는
하나의 만족을 찾아내는 것이어야 한다. 그리고
스케이트 타는 남자, 춤추는 여자, 빗질하는
여자여도 된다. 마음의 연기의 시는.

The Poem of Our Climate

I
Clear water in a brilliant bowl,
Pink and white carnations. The light
In the room more like a snowy air,
Reflecting snow. A newly-fallen snow
At the end of winter when afternoons return.
Pink and white carnations – one desires
So much more than that. The day itself
Is simplified: a bowl of white,
Cold, a cold porcelain, low and round,
With nothing more than the carnations there.

II
Say even that this complete simplicity
Stripped one of all one's torments, concealed
The evilly compounded, vital I
And made it fresh in a world of white,
A world of clear water, brilliant-edged,
Still one would want more, one would need more,
More than a world of white and snowy scents.

III
There would still remain the never-resting mind,
So that one would want to escape, come back
To what had been so long composed.
The imperfect is our paradise.
Note that, in this bitterness, delight,
Since the imperfect is so hot in us,
Lies in flawed words and stubborn sounds.

우리 풍토의 시

I
찬란한 사발에 담긴 맑은 물,
핑크 빛 흰 빛 카네이션. 눈을 반사하는
하얀 공기 같은 방 안의
햇빛. 오후가 돌아왔을 때
겨울의 끝 무렵 갓 내린 눈.
핑크 빛 흰 빛 카네이션— 우리는
그것 이상의 것을 바란다. 그 날 자체가
단순화된다. 하얀 빛의 사발,
찬, 하나의 싸늘한, 납작하고 둥근 자기와
오직 카네이션만이 거기에 있는 것으로.

II
말하라, 이 완전한 단순이 우리에게서
모든 인간의 고뇌를 벗기고
악으로 뭉쳐진 생명력 넘치는 나를 숨겨,
흰 빛 세계 안에서 그것을 신선하게 했다고,
맑은 물, 찬란한 테두리의 세계로,
여전히 우리는 그 이상을 바라고, 그 이상을 필요로 한다,
하얀 눈 같은 향기의 세계 이상을.

III
거기엔 여전히 결코 안주하지 않는 마음이 있다,
그래서 우리는 도망치려 하고,
오랜 동안 만들어진 것에 돌아가려고 한다.
불완전한 것이 우리의 낙원이다.
보아라 불완전한 것이 우리 안에서 아주 뜨겁기 때문에
이 가혹한 것 속에, 즐거움이 놓여 있음을,
흠 있는 언어와 고집스런 음향으로 쓰여진.

The Snow Man

One must have a mind of winter
To regard the frost and the boughs
Of the pine-trees crusted with snow;

And have been cold a long time
To behold the junipers shagged with ice,
The spruces rough in the distant glitter

Of the January sun; and not to think
Of any misery in the sound of the wind,
In the sound of a few leaves,

Which is the sound of the land
Full of the same wind
That is blowing in the same bare place
For the listener, who listens in the snow,
And, nothing himself, beholds
Nothing that is not there and the nothing that is.

눈 사람

사람은 겨울의 마음을 가졌음에 틀림없다,
눈이 더덕더덕 얼어붙은 소나무의
큰 가지나 서리를 생각한다.

그리고 오랜 동안 추위 속에 있어왔음이 틀림없다.
얼음으로 녹초가 된 로뎀나무나
1월 태양의 아득한 광채 속에서

거칠게 드러나는 가문비나무를 본다,
그리고 바람 소리나 몇 잎 나무 이파리 소리에
어떠한 비참함도 생각지 않는다,

그 소리는 똑 같은 황량한 장소에서
불고 있는 똑 같은 바람 가득찬
땅에서의 소리이다.

귀 기울이는 자에게, 그는 눈 속에서
귀 기울이며, 무로서의 자신이
거기에 없는 무와 거기에 있는 무를 본다.

Thirteen Ways of Looking at a Blackbird

I
Among twenty snowy mountains,
The only moving thing
Was the eye of the black bird.

II
I was of three minds,
Like a tree
In which there are three blackbirds.

III
The blackbird whirled in the autumn winds.
It was a small part of the pantomime.

IV
A man and a woman
Are one.
A man and a woman and a blackbird
Are one.

V
I do not know which to prefer,
The beauty of inflections
Or the beauty of innuendoes,
The blackbird whistling
Or just after.

찌르레기를 보는 열세가지 모습

I
눈 오는 스무개 산 속에서,
단 하나 움직이는 것은
찌르레기의 눈이었다.

II
나는 세 마음이었다,
세 마리 찌르레기가 있는
나무처럼.

III
찌르레기는 가을 바람 속에서 선회하였다
그것은 팬터마임의 작은 일부였다.

IV
남자와 여자는
하나다.
남자와 여자와 찌르레기는
하나다.

V
나는 어느 쪽을 취할지 모르겠다.
음조의 변화의 미인가
또는 암시의 미인가,
한참 지저귈 때의 찌르레기인가.
또는 막 그쳤을 때의 그 새인가.

VI
Icicles filled the long window
With barbaric glass.
The shadow of the blackbird
Crossed it, to and fro.
The mood
Traced in the shadow
An indecipherable cause.

VII
O thin men of Haddam,
Why do you imagine golden birds?
Do you not see how the blackbird
Walks around the feet
Of the women about you?

VIII
I know noble accents
And lucid, inescapable rhythms;
But I know, too,
That the blackbird is involved
In what I know.

IX
When the blackbird flew out of sight,
It marked the edge
Of one of many circles.

X
At the sight of blackbirds
Flying in a green light,
Even the bawds of euphony
Would cry out sharply.

VI
고드름이 긴 창문을 야만스럽게 유리에 비쳐 가득 채웠다.
찌르레기의 그림자가
그 창을 이리저리 지났다.
그 기분은
그림자 속에서
해독할 수 없는 원인을 더듬었다.

VII
아, 하담의 야윈 사람들이여,
무엇 때문에 금빛 새들을 상상하는가.
너희들 근처의 여인들의
발 주위를 찌르레기가
걷는 것이 보이지 않는가.

VIII
나는 안다, 고상한 어조나
분명하고 확실한 리듬을.
그러나 이것도 안다,
내가 아는 세계에는
찌르레기가 포함되어 있는 것을.

IX
찌르레기가 날아서 보이지 않을 때,
그 지점은
많은 원 중의 한 원의 그 가.

X
푸른 빛 속을 나는
찌르레기 들을 보면,
고운 음조의 갈보도
날카롭게 소리 지를 것이다.

XI
He rode over Connecticut
In a glass coach.
Once, a fear pierced him,
In that he mistook
The shadow of his equipage
For blackbirds.

XII
The river is moving.
The blackbird must be flying.

XIII
It was evening all afternoon.
It was snowing
And it was going to snow.
The blackbird sat
In the cedar-limbs.

XI
그는 코네티컷을
유리 마차를 타고 지났다.
언젠가 공포에 질렸다,
그는
마차의 그림자를
찌르레기로 착각했기 때문에.

XII
강은 움직이고 있다.
찌르레기가 날고 있음에 틀림 없다.

XIII
오후는 계속 저녁이었다.
눈이 오고 있었고
앞으로 눈이 오려고 했었다.
찌르레기는 앉아 있었다
삼나무 가지에.

Langston Hughes (1902-1967)

James Mercer Langston Hughes was born February 1, 1902, in Joplin, Missouri. His parents divorced when he was a young child, and his father moved to Mexico. He was raised by his grandmother until he was thirteen, when he moved to Lincoln, Illinois, to live with his mother and her husband, before the family eventually settled in Cleveland, Ohio. It was in Lincoln that Hughes began writing poetry. After graduating from high school, he spent a year in Mexico followed by a year at Columbia University in New York City. During this time, he held odd jobs such as assistant cook, launderer, and busboy. He also travelled to Africa and Europe working as a seaman. In November 1924, he moved to Washington, D. C. Hughes's first book of poetry, *The Weary Blues*, (1926) was published by Alfred A. Knopf in 1926. He finished his college education at Lincoln University in Pennsylvania three years later. In 1930 his first novel, *Not Without Laughter*, (1930) won the Harmon gold medal for literature.

His life and work were enormously important in shaping the artistic contributions of the Harlem Renaissance of the 1920s. Unlike other notable black poets of the period — Claude McKay, Jean Toomer, and Countee Cullen — Hughes refused to differentiate between his personal experience and the common experience of black America. He wanted to tell the stories of his people in ways that reflected their actual culture, including both their suffering and their love of music, laughter, and language itself.

The critic Donald B. Gibson noted in the introduction to

Modern Black Poets: A Collection of Critical Essays (1973) that Hughes "differed from most of his predecessors among black poets . . . in that he addressed his poetry to the people, specifically to black people. During the twenties when most American poets were turning inward, writing obscure and esoteric poetry to an ever decreasing audience of readers, Hughes was turning outward, using language and themes, attitudes and ideas familiar to anyone who had the ability simply to read . . . Until the time of his death, he spread his message humorously — though always seriously — to audiences throughout the country, having read his poetry to more people (possibly) than any other American poet."

Langston Hughes died of complications from prostate cancer on May 22, 1967, in New York City. In his memory, his residence at 20 East 127th Street in Harlem has been given landmark status by the New York City Preservation Commission, and East 127th Street has been renamed "Langston Hughes Place."

Afro-American Fragment

So long,
So far away
Is Africa.
Not even memories alive
Save those that history books create,
Save those that songs
Beat back into the blood–
Beat out of blood with words sad-sung
In strange un-Negro tongue–
So long,
So far away
Is Africa.

Subdued and time-lost
Are the drums–and yet
Through some vast mist of race
There comes this song
I do not understand,
This song of atavistic land,
Of bitter yearnings lost
Without a place–
So long,
So far away
Is Africa's
Dark face.

흑인 단장

저 옛날
저 멀리에 있는
아프리카
아무런 기억조차 살아 있지 않아
역사책이 조작한 것들을 제외한다면
핏속으로 저미는 노래—
낯선 비흑인의 어투로
불리는 슬픈 가사를 가진—
노래들을 제외한다면
저 옛날
저 멀리에 있는
아프리카.

북소리 이미 사라지고
좋은 시절 잃었어도
널리 잡다하게 퍼진 인종 따라
흘러나오는 이 노래
알 수 없어
이미 사라져버린
쓰라린 동경을 담은
격세유전의 이 노래
정처 없는 땅의 이 노래를
저 옛날
저 멀리에 있는
아프리카의
어두운 얼굴.

As I Grew Older

It was a long time ago.
I have almost forgotten my dream.
But it was there then,
In front of me,
Bright like a sun —
My dream.
And then the wall rose,
Rose slowly,
Slowly,
Between me and my dream.
Rose until it touched the sky —
The wall.
Shadow.
I am black.
I lie down in the shadow.
No longer the light of my dream before me,
Above me.
Only the thick wall.
Only the shadow.
My hands!
My dark hands!
Break through the wall!
Find my dream!
Help me to shatter this darkness,
To smash this night,
To break this shadow
Into a thousand lights of sun,
Into a thousand whirling dreams
Of sun!

나 늙어갈 때

오래 전에
하마터면 나는 내 꿈을 잊을 뻔 했다.
하지만 그것은 그 때
내 앞에서
태양처럼 빛나고 있었다.
나의 꿈.
그리고 나서 벽이 일어섰다.
천천히
천천히 일어서서
나와 내 꿈 사이를 가로막고
하늘에 닿을 때까지 솟아올랐다.
그 벽.
그림자.
나는 검둥이다.
나는 그림자 아래 눕는다.
더 이상 내 꿈의 불빛은 내 앞에 없다.
내 위로는
오로지 두꺼운 벽.
오로지 어두운 그늘.
나의 손들!
나의 검은 손들!
벽을 두들긴다!
내 꿈을 찾기 위해!
이 어둠을 쳐부수도록 도와주오.
이 밤을 깨뜨리고.
이 그림자를 부수고
눈부신 태양의 빛살.
소용돌이치는 태양의 꿈 앞에
나설 수 있도록!

Harlem

What happens to a dream deferred?

Does it dry up
like a raisin in the sun?
Or fester like a sore—
And then run?
Does it stink like rotten meat?
Or crust and sugar over—
like a syrupy sweet?

Maybe it just sags
like a heavy load.

Or does it explode?

할렘

미뤄진 꿈에 어떤 일이 일어나지?

건포도처럼
햇볕에 말라버리나?
아니면 종기처럼
곪아 터져버리나?
썩은 고기처럼 악취가 나나?
아니면 굳어버린 달콤한 시럽처럼
껍질 위에 설탕만 남나?

아마 그것은 무거운 짐처럼
처져버릴지도.

아니면 폭탄처럼 터져버리나?

I, Too

I, too, sing America.

I am the darker brother.
They send me to eat in the kitchen
When company comes,
But I laugh,
And eat well,
And grow strong.

Tomorrow,
I'll be at the table
When company comes.
Nobody'll dare
Say to me,
"Eat in the kitchen,"
Then.

Besides,
They'll see how beautiful I am
And be ashamed—

I, too, am America.

나도

나도 미국을 노래한다.

난 더 검은 피부를 가진 형제이다.
손님이 오면,
그들은 내게 부엌에 가 먹으라 하나
난 웃고,
잘 먹으며,
점점 강해진다.

내일.
손님이 오면.
나는 식탁에 앉아있으리.
아무도 감히
내게
"부엌에서 먹거라."라고
말하지 못할 것이다.

더욱이,
그들은 내가 얼마나 아름다운 사람인가를 알게 되고,
부끄러워할 것이다.

나도 미국을 노래한다.

Negro Speaks of Rivers

I've known rivers:
I've known rivers ancient as the world and older than the flow of human blood in human veins.

My soul has grown deep like the rivers.

I bathed in the Euphrates when dawns were young.
I built my hut near the Congo and it lulled me to sleep.
I looked upon the Nile and raised the pyramids above it.
I heard the singing of the Mississippi when Abe Lincoln went down to New Orleans, and I've seen its muddy bosom turn all golden in the sunset.

I've known rivers:
Ancient, dusky rivers.

My soul has grown deep like the rivers.

검둥이, 강을 말하다

나는 강들을 알고 있다.
나는 이 세계만큼이나 오래되고 인간의 정맥 속 흐르는 피보다
더 오래 흘러온 강들을 알고 있다.

나의 영혼은 그 강들만큼 깊게 자랐다.

난 동이 틀 때 유프라테스 강에서 목욕했다.
콩고 근처에 내 오두막을 지어놨는데 그것이 나를 진정시켜 편안히
　　잠들게 했다.
나는 나일 강을 지켜봤고 그 강위에 피라미드를 세웠다.
나는 에이브 링컨이 뉴올리언스에 도달했을 때
미시시피 강의 노래를 들었고, 그리고 그 강의 진흙투성이
가슴이 해질녘 모두 황금빛으로 변하는 것을 보았다.

나는 강들을 알고 있다.
아주 오래된, 거뭇한 강들을.

내 영혼은 그 강들만큼 깊게 자랐다.

Theme for English B

The instructor said,

Go home and write
a page tonight.
And let that page come out of you—
Then, it will be true.

I wonder if it's that simple?
I am twenty-two, colored, born in Winston-Salem.
I went to school there, then Durham, then here
to this college on the hill above Harlem.
I am the only colored student in my class.
The steps from the hill lead down into Harlem,
through a park, then I cross St. Nicholas,
Eighth Avenue, Seventh, and I come to the Y,
the Harlem Branch Y, where I take the elevator
up to my room, sit down, and write this page:

It's not easy to know what is true for you or me
at twenty-two, my age. But I guess I'm what
I feel and see and hear, Harlem, I hear you.
hear you, hear me—we two—you, me, talk on this page.
(I hear New York, too.) Me—who?

Well, I like to eat, sleep, drink, and be in love.
I like to work, read, learn, and understand life.
I like a pipe for a Christmas present,
or records—Bessie, bop, or Bach.
I guess being colored doesn't make me not like

영어 B반을 위한 주제

선생은 말했다.

집에 가서 오늘밤
글 한 쪽을 쓰거라.
그 글은 꼭 네 것이어야 해--
그래야 진짜 글이 될 것이야.

그게 그렇게 간단한 일인지 궁금했다.
나는 스물두 살, 유색인종에 윈스턴 세일럼 출신이다.
그곳에서 학교를 다녔고, 그 다음은 더햄, 그리고 이곳
할렘가 위쪽 언덕에 있는 대학에 다닌다.
난 우리 반의 유일한 유색인종 학생이다.
언덕 아래로 난 계단은 할렘 쪽으로 이어지고
공원을 지나 성 니콜라스를 가로지른다.
8번가, 7번가, 그리고서 나는 Y에 이른다
할렘가에 있는 Y, 그곳에서 난 엘리베이터를 타고
내 방으로 향하며, 앉아서, 이 글을 쓴다.

당신이나 나이 스물두 살인 나에게 어떤 게 진실인지
아는 것은 쉽지 않다. 하지만 내가 추측하건대
내가 느끼고 보고 듣는 것이 나다, 할렘, 나는 네 소리를 들어.
너를 듣고, 나를 듣지—우리 둘—너와, 나, 이 글에서 이야기하지.
(나는 뉴욕 또한 들어.) 내가 누구냐고?

글쎄, 나는 먹고 자고 마시고 사랑하길 좋아하지.
일하고 읽고 배우고, 그리고 삶을 이해하길 좋아해.
크리스마스 선물로 파이프나
베시, 밥, 바흐의 레코드도 좋아하지.
내가 유색인종이기 때문에 다른 인종이 좋아하는 것들을

the same things other folks like who are other races.
So will my page be colored that I write?
Being me, it will not be white.
But it will be
a part of you, instructor.
You are white—
yet a part of me, as I am a part of you.
That's American.
Sometimes perhaps you don't want to be a part of me.
Nor do I often want to be a part of you.
But we are, that's true!
As I learn from you,
I guess you learn from me—
although you're older—and white—
and somewhat more free.

This is my page for English B.

좋아하지 않게 되는 것은 아니라고 생각해.
그렇다면 내가 쓰는 글은 유색이 되나?
나의 일부이기에, 하얗지는 않겠지.
하지만 이것은
선생, 당신의 일부일 수도 있어.
당신은 백인이야—
하지만 나의 일부이며, 나는 당신의 일부이기도하지.
미국인이니까.
때때로 당신은 나의 일부가 되는 것을 원하지 않을 수 있어.
나 역시 가끔은 당신의 일부가 되는 것을 원하지 않지.
하지만 우리는 존재하고, 이것은 진실이야!
나는 당신을 통해 배우고,
당신은 나를 통해 배운다고 생각해—
당신이 나이가 많고, 백인이고
어디인가 자유롭긴 하지만.

이것이 영어 B반을 위한 내 글이야.

Theodore Roethke (1908-1963)

On May 25, 1908, Theodore Roethke was born in Saginaw, Michigan. As a child, he spent much time in the greenhouse owned by his father and uncle. His impressions of the natural world contained there would later profoundly influence the subjects and imagery of his verse. Roethke graduated magna cum laude from the University of Michigan in 1929. He later took a few graduate classes at Michigan and Harvard, but was unhappy in school. His first book, *Open House* (1941), took ten years to write and was critically acclaimed upon its publication. He went on to publish sparingly but his reputation grew with each new collection, including *The Waking* which was awarded the Pulitzer Prize in 1954.

He admired the writing of such poets as Emerson, Thoreau, Whitman, Blake, and Wordsworth, as well as Yeats and Dylan Thomas. Stylistically his work ranged from witty poems in strict meter and regular stanzas to free verse poems full of mystical and surrealistic imagery. At all times, however, the natural world in all its mystery, beauty, fierceness, and sensuality, is close by, and the poems are possessed of an intense lyricism.

Roethke had close literary friendships with fellow poets W. H. Auden, Louise Bogan, Stanley Kunitz, and William Carlos Williams. He taught at various colleges and universities, including Lafayette, Pennsylvania State, and Bennington, and worked last at the University of Washington, where he was mentor to a generation of Northwest poets that included David Wagoner, Carolyn Kizer, and Richard Hugo. Theodore Roethke died on August 1, 1963.

Dolor

I have known the inexorable sadness of pencils,
Neat in their boxes, dolor of pad and paper weight,
All the misery of manilla folders and mucilage,
Desolation in immaculate public places,
Lonely reception room, lavatory, switchboard,
The unalterable pathos of basin and pitcher,
Ritual of multigraph, paper-clip, comma,
Endless duplicaton of lives and objects.
And I have seen dust from the walls of institutions,
Finer than flour, alive, more dangerous than silica,
Sift, almost invisible, through long afternoons of tedium,
Dropping a fine film on nails and delicate eyebrows,
Glazing the pale hair, the duplicate grey standard faces.

비애

곽 속에 깨끗하게 들어있는 연필들의 가혹한 슬픔을,
압지와 문진의 슬픔을, 서류철과
마닐라 폴더와 고무풀의 온갖 슬픔을,
깔끔한 공공장소,
인적 없는 접대실, 화장실, 교환대의 적막을.
대야와 물병의 변함 없는 애수를,
식자인쇄기, 종이집게, 구두점의 의식을,
생명과 물체들의 끊임없는 동질화를 나는 알고 있다.
그리고 공공건물의 벽에서 밀가루보다 곱고,
살아 있어, 규토보다 더 무시무시한 먼지가 거의 보이지 않게,
지루한 오후의 권태 속으로 흘러내려 손톱과 섬세한 눈썹 위에
고운 막을 떨어뜨리며, 창백한 머리와
똑같은 창백한 표준형 얼굴들을 번들번들하게 하는 것을 보았다.

In a Dark Time

In a dark time, the eye begins to see,
I meet my shadow in the deepening shade;
I hear my echo in the echoing wood—
A lord of nature weeping to a tree.
I live between the heron and the wren,
Beasts of the hill and serpents of the den.

What's madness but nobility of soul
At odds with circumstance? The day's on fire!
I know the purity of pure despair,
My shadow pinned against a sweating wall.
That place among the rocks—is it a cave,
Or a winding path? The edge is what I have.

A steady storm of correspondences!
A night flowing with birds, a ragged moon,
And in broad day the midnight come again!
A man goes far to find out what he is—
Death of the self in a long, tearless night,
All natural shapes blazing unnatural light.

Dark, dark my light, and darker my desire.
My soul, like some heat-maddened summer fly,
Keeps buzzing at the sill. Which I is I?
A fallen man, I climb out of my fear.
The mind enters itself, and God the mind,
And one is One, free in the tearing wind.

어둠의 시간에

어둠의 시간에, 눈은 보기 시작하고,
나는 짙어가는 그늘 속에서 내 그림자를 만난다.
메아리치는 숲 속에서 나의 메아리를 듣는다. —
나무에 눈물 짓는 자연의 주의 목소리를.
나는 왜가리와 굴뚝새 사이에서 산다,
산의 짐승들과 굴의 뱀들 사이에서.

상황과 싸우는 광증은
영혼의 고결이 아니고 무엇이냐. 낮은 불탄다.
나는 순수한 절망의 순수를 안다,
땀 흘리는 벽에 꽂힌 내 그림자를.
바위와 바위 사위 — 그것은 동굴이냐,
아니면 구불구불한 길이냐, 내가 가진 것은 그 가장자리이다.

조응의 한결같은 소란! —
밤은 새들과 이지러진 달과 함께 흐르고,
대낮에 다시 한밤중이 온다.
사람은 그가 무엇인가를 알기 위하여 멀리 간다 —
긴 눈물 없는 밤의 자아의 죽음,
온갖 자연의 삼라만상이 부자연한 빛으로 불탄다.

어둡다, 내 빛이 어둡다, 내 욕망은 더 어둡다.
내 영혼은, 열기에 미친 여름 파리처럼
문지방에서 계속 웅웅댄다. 어느 내가 '나'냐.
한 죄인, 나는 나의 두려움에서 벗어난다.
마음은 그 자체 속으로, 신은 마음 속으로 들어간다.
사람은 사나운 바람 속에서 자유로이 신과 결합한다.

My Papa's Waltz

The whiskey on your breath
Could make a small boy dizzy;
But I hung on like death:
Such waltzing was not easy.

We romped until the pans
Slid from the kitchen shelf;
My mother's countenance
Could not unfrown itself.

The hand that held my wrist
Was battered on one knuckle;
At every step you missed
My right ear scraped a buckle.

You beat time on my head
With a palm caked hard by dirt,
Then waltzed me off to bed
Still clinging to your shirt.

내 아버지의 왈츠

당신의 숨에서 묻어나는 위스키 향기는요
한 작은 소년을 어지럽게 만들었죠.
하지만 난 필사적으로 매달려요
그런 왈츠는 쉽지 않죠.

우리는 즐겁게 뛰어 놀았어요
부엌 찬장에 있는 후라이팬들이 미끄러졌네요
우리 엄마의 표정은요
그대로 찌푸려졌네요

내 손목을 잡은 손으로다가
손가락 마디를 부딪혀요
당신이 스텝을 놓칠 때마다
내 귀는 버클에 긁혔어요

당신은 나의 머리를 때리지요
흙 범벅이 된 손으로
그리곤 춤을 추며 침대로 날 데려다줬지요
여전히 당신의 셔츠에 매달려 있는 채로

Open House

My secrets cry aloud.
I have no need for tongue.
My heart keeps open house,
My doors are widely swung.
An epic of the eyes
My love, with no disguise.

My truths are all foreknown,
This anguish self-revealed.
I'm naked to the bone,
With nakedness my shield.
Myself is what I wear:
I keep the spirit spare.

The anger will endure,
The deed will speak the truth
In language strict and pure.
I stop the lying mouth:
Rage warps my clearest cry
To witless agony.

열린 집

나의 비밀은 큰 소리로 외친다.
내겐 혀가 필요 없다.
내 마음은 열린 집,
내 문은 넓게 열려 있다.
그것은 나의 눈의 서사시.
아무 위장도 없는 나의 사랑.

나의 진리는 모두 미리 알려진다,
이 고뇌도 스스로 드러난다.
나는 뼈 속까지 가린 것이 없다,
벌거벗은 것이 나의 방패.
내 자신이 나의 옷.
나는 정신을 쓰지 않는다.

분노는 존속하리라,
행위가 진실을 말하리라,
거짓 없는 순수한 말로.
나는 거짓말 하는 입을 틀어막는다.
분노는 나의 아주 맑은 외침을 비틀어
어리석은 고뇌로 이끈다.

The Rose(4)

I live with rocks, their weeds,
Their filmy fringes of green, their harsh
Edges, their holes
Cut by the sea-slime, far from the crash
Of the long swell,
The oily, tar-laden walls
Of the toppling waves,
Where the salmon ease their way into the kelp beds,
And the sea rearranges itself among the small islands.

Near this rose, in this grove of sun-parched, wind-warped madronas,
Among the half-dead trees, I came upon the true ease of myself,
As if another man appeared out of the depths of my being,
And I stood outside myself,
Beyond becoming and perishing,
A something wholly other,
As if I swayed out on the wildest wave alive,
And yet was still.
And I rejoiced in being what I was:
In the lilac change, the whit reptilian calm,
In the bird beyond the bough, the single one
With all the air to greet him as he flies,
The dolphin rising from the darkening waves;

And in this rose, this rose in the sea-wind,
Rooted in stone, keeping the whole of light,
Gathering into itself sound and silence–
Mine and the sea-wind's.

장미(4)

나는 바위와 더불어 살고, 거기에 난 잡초와 함께 산다,
그 푸른 엷은 가장자리와 그 거친
가장자리와, 긴 굽이치는 물결의
부서지는 소리에서 멀리 떠난 바다의 점액으로 에여파진
바위의 구멍과,
부서져 떨어지는 파도의
기름 묻고, 타르가 달라붙은 벽과 함께,
연어가 해초벌로 천천히 들어가는 그 곳에서,
그리고 바다가 작은 섬들 사이에서 재정비되는 그 곳에서,

햇볕에 그을리고, 바람에 휜 석남화 숲 속 이 장미 가까이에서,
반쯤 죽은 나무들 사이에서 나는 진정으로 몸의 편안을 알았다.
마치 또 다른 한 사람이 내 존재의 밑바닥에서 나타난 것처럼,
그리고 나는 내 몸 밖에 서 있다.
생성과 멸망을 벗어난 저편에,
전혀 딴 것이 되어,
마치 생생한 거친 파도 위에 흔들려 나와
그러나 정직한 듯이.
그리하여 나는 있는 그대로의 내가 좋았다,
라일락의 변화와, 파충류의 흰 정적과,
가지 너머의 새, 날면
전체 대기가 환영하는 그 한 마리 새와,
시꺼먼 파도에서 솟아 오르는 돌고래가 좋았다,

그리고 이 장미, 해풍 속의 이 장미,
돌에 뿌리 박고, 빛의 모든 것을 간직하고,
소리와 정적을 혼자 차지하고 있는 이 장미가 —
그것은 나의 것, 해풍의 것.

The Voice

One feather is a bird,
I claim; one tree, a wood;
In her low voice I heard
More than a mortal should;
And so I stood apart,
Hidden in my own heart.

And yet I roamed out where
Those notes went, like the bird,
Whose thin song hung in air,
Diminished, yet still heard:
I lived with open sound,
Aloft, and on the ground.

That ghost was my own choice,
The shy cerulean bird;
It sang with her true voice,
And it was I who heard
A slight voice reply;
I heard; and only I.

Desire exults the ear:
Bird, girl, and ghostly tree,
The earth, the solid air—
Their slow song sang in me;
The long noon pulsed away,
Like any summer day.

목소리

나는 주장한다, 깃털 하나가
한 마리 새라고. 나무 하나가 숲이라고.
그녀의 낮은 목소리에서 나는 들었다.
한 인간이 들을 수 있는 이상의 것을.
그래서 나는 떨어져 서서,
내 마음 속에 숨었다.

그러나 나는 어슬렁 거닐어 나갔다,
그 곡조들이 새처럼 날아간 곳으로,
그 희미한 노래는 공중에 걸려,
줄어들었으나, 여전히 들렸다.
나는 허공의 음향과 함께 살았다,
공중에서, 지상에서.

저 환영, 수줍은 하늘색 새는,
내 자신이 택한 것.
그것은 제 참 목소리로 노래했고,
나는 하나의 희미한 목소리가
답하는 것을 들었다.
나는 들었다. 그리고 나 뿐이었다.

욕망은 귀를 즐겁게 한다,
새, 소녀, 그리고 유령 같은 나무,
대지, 농밀한 대기 —
그것들의 노래는 내 속에서 천천히 노래했다.
긴 대낮은 고동치며 지나갔다,
여느 여름 날처럼.

Gary Snyder (1930-)

He has published numerous books of poetry and prose, including *Danger on Peaks* (2005) *The Gary Snyder Reader* (1999); *Mountains and Rivers Without End* (1997); *No Nature: New and Selected Poems* (1993), which was a finalist for the National Book Award; *The Practice of the Wild* (1990); *Left Out in the Rain, New Poems 1947-1985*; *Axe Handles* (1983), for which he received an American Book Award; *Turtle Island* (1974), which won the Pulitzer Prize for poetry; *Regarding Wave* (1970); and *Myths & Texts* (1960).

Snyder has received an American Academy of Arts and Letters award, the Bollingen Prize, a Guggenheim Foundation fellowship, the Bess Hokin Prize and the Levinson Prize from Poetry, the Robert Kirsch Lifetime Achievement Award from the Los Angeles Times, the Ruth Lilly Poetry Prize, and the Shelley Memorial Award. Snyder was elected a Chancellor of the Academy of American Poets in 2003.

The author and editor Stewart Brand once wrote: "Gary Snyder's poetry addresses the life-planet identification with unusual simplicity of style and complexity of effect." According to Jody Norton, this simplicity and complexity derives from Snyder's use of natural imagery (geographical formations, flora, and fauna) in his poems. Such imagery can be both sensual at a personal level yet universal and generic in nature. Snyder has always maintained that his personal sensibility arose from his interest in Native Americans and their involvement with nature and knowledge of it; indeed, their ways seemed to resonate with his own. And he has sought something akin to this through Buddhist practices, Yamabushi initiation, and other experiences and involvements. However, since his youth he has been quite literate, and he has written about his appreciation of writers of similar sensibilities, like D. H. Lawrence, William Butler Yeats, and some of the great ancient Chinese poets. William Carlos Williams was another influence, especially on Snyder's earliest published work. Starting in high school, Snyder read and loved the work of Robinson Jeffers, his predecessor in poetry of the landscape of the American West; but, whereas Jeffers valued nature over humankind, Snyder saw humankind as part of nature.

Snyder was the recipient of the 2012 Wallace Stevens Award for lifetime achievement by the Academy of American Poets. He is a professor of English at the University of California, Davis.

For All

Ah to be alive
on a mid-September morn
fording a stream
barefoot, pants rolled up,
holding boots, pack on,
sunshine, ice in the shallows,
northern rockies.

Rustle and shimmer of icy creek waters
stones turn underfoot, small and hard as toes
cold nose dripping
singing inside
creek music, heart music,
smell of sun on gravel.

I pledge allegiance

I pledge allegiance to the soil
of Turtle Island,
and to the beings who thereon dwell
one ecosystem
in diversity
under the sun
With joyful interpenetration for all.

모두에게

북쪽의 록키산맥
햇빛, 얕은 곳은 빙판
장화를 들고, 배낭을 등에 지고,
맨발로, 바지를 걷어 올리고
여울을 건너는
구월 중순 아침에
아, 살아 있음이여.

얼음이 덮인 시냇물은 재잘거리고 빛나며
발 아래 뒤엎어지는 자갈들, 발가락처럼 작고 단단하고
찬 콧물이 흐르고
속으로 노래하며
시냇물 노래, 가슴의 노래,
자갈 위의 햇빛의 냄새.

나는 충성을 맹세한다.

나는 충성을 맹세한다 거북섬 안의
온 땅에게,
그리고 그곳에 살고 있는 온 생물이
하나의 생태계로
다양하게
하늘 아래서
모두가 기쁜 공존 안에서 살 수 있도록.

Hay for the Horses

He had driven half the night
From far down San Joaquin
Through Mariposa, up the
Dangerous Mountain roads,
And pulled in at eight a.m.
With his big truckload of hay
          behind the barn.
With winch and ropes and hooks
We stacked the bales up clean
To splintery redwood rafters
High in the dark, flecks of alfalfa
Whirling through shingle-cracks of light,
Itch of haydust in the
          sweaty shirt and shoes.
At lunchtime under Black oak
Out in the hot corral,
—-The old mare nosing lunchpails,
Grasshoppers crackling in the weeds—-
"I'm sixty-eight" he said,
"I first bucked hay when I was seventeen.
I thought, that day I started,
I sure would hate to do this all my life.
And dammit, that's just what
I've gone and done."

말들을 위한 건초

그는 저 아래 샌와킨에서
위험한 산길 타고
마리포사를 지나
밤새 북으로 달려
아침 여덟시
마초를 가득 실은 트럭을
　　　　곳간 뒤에 대었다.
권양기와 밧줄과 고리로
우리는 그 마초를 높이 쌓아올렸다.
가시 박힌 주목 서까래
그 위 어둠 속에서 알팔파 티끌들이
지붕 널 틈으로 들어오는 햇볕 안에서 뱅글거리고
땀에 젖은 속옷과 신발 속의
　　　　건초 티끌로 가렵다.
무더운 축사 밖
큰 떡갈나무 아래서 점심시간에
—늙은 숫말이 점심그릇에 코를 들이밀며
귀뚜라미가 풀 속에서 귀뚤거리는데—
"나는 예순 여덟입니다." 하고 그가 말했다.
"열일곱살에 처음으로 건초를 날랐는데
그 일 시작하던 날
이 일을 평생하게 되는게 아닌가 싶었는데
빌어먹을, 이 짓을
여지껏 하고 있단 말입니다."

Prayer for the Great Family

Gratitude to Mother Earth, sailing through night and day–
and to her soil: rich, rare, and sweet
in our minds so be it.

Gratitude to Plants, the sun-facing light-changing leaf
and fine root-hairs; standing still through wind
and rain; their dance is in the flowing spiral grain
in our minds so be it.

Gratitude to Air, bearing the soaring Swift and the silent
Owl at dawn. Breath of our song
clear spirit breeze
in our minds so be it.

Gratitude to Wild Beings, our brothers, teaching secrets,
freedoms and ways; who share with us their milk;
self-complete, brave, and aware
in our minds so be it.

Gratitude to Water: clouds, lakes, rivers, glaciers;
holding or releasing; streaming through all
our bodies salty seas
in our minds so be it.

Gratitude to the Sun: blinding pulsing light through
trunks of trees, through mists, warming caves where
bears and snakes sleep–he who wakes us–
in our minds so be it.

위대한 가족에게 드리는 기도

밤낮을 계속해서 항해하는 어머니 지구에게 —
그리고 비옥하고 귀하고 사랑스러운 그녀의 땅에게 감사드립니다
우리 마음도 그렇게 되게 하소서.

해를 향하고 빛을 변형시키는 잎과
섬세한 뿌리털 ; 비바람 속에서
묵묵히 서 있으며 ; 그들의 흐르는 춤이 나선형의 결을 이루는
식물에게 감사드립니다
우리 마음도 그렇게 되게 하소서.

치솟는 칼새며 새벽의 말 없는 부엉이를 지탱해 주는
공기에게 감사드립니다. 우리 노래의 호흡
맑은 령의 미풍
우리 마음도 그렇게 되게 하소서.

우리의 형제 자매로, 비밀스러움, 자유 그리고
여러 길들을 보여주며 ; 그들의 젖을 우리에게 나눠주며 ;
스스로 완전하며, 용감하고 깨인 야성의 존재들에게 감사드립니다
우리 마음도 그렇게 되게 하소서.

구름, 호수, 강, 빙하 ;
보존하고 풀어주며 ; 우리 몸 속의 소금기 있는 바다를 흐르는
물에게 감사드립니다
우리 마음도 그렇게 되게 하소서.

율동하는 눈부신 빛으로
나무 등걸 속을, 안개 속을 통하고, — 우리를 깨우며 —
곰과 뱀들이 잠자는 동굴을 쬐는
태양에게 감사드립니다
우리 마음도 그렇게 되게 하소서.

Gratitude to the Great Sky
who holds billions of stars–and goes yet beyond that–
beyond all powers, and thoughts
and yet is within us–
Grandfather Space.
The Mind is his Wife

so be it.

after a Mohawk Prayer

수억의 별들을 담고 — 그리고 그 너머로 가며 —
모든 힘과, 생각 저쪽에 있으면서
우리 안에 있는 —
위대한 하늘에 감사합니다. 할아버지의 허공.
마음이 그의 아내이다.

그렇게 되게 하소서.

모학 기도문 식으로.

Ripples on the Surface

“Ripples on the surface of water
were silver salmon passing under — different
from the sorts of ripples caused by breezes”

A scudding plume on the wave —
a humpback whale is
breaking out in air up
gulping herring
    — Nature not a book, but a performance, a
high old culture.

Ever-fresh events
scraped out, rubbed out, and used, used, again —
the braided channels of the rivers
hidden under fields of grass —

The vast wild
    the house, alone.
the little house in the wild,
    the wild in the house.

both forgotten.

No nature.

Both together, one big empty house.

수면의 파문

"아래로 은빛 연어가 지나가는 —
수면의 파문은 —미풍으로
생기는 파문과는 다르다"

파도 위에서 질주하는 물기둥은—
곱사등이 고래가
청어를 삼키며
숨쉬기 위해 공중 위로
돌파하는 것
　　— 자연은 책이 아닌, 연기, 하나의
뛰어난 오랜 문화

언제나 새로운 사건들
비벼서 벗기고, 문질러 지우고, 그렇게 이용하고, 이용하고, 또 다시—
풀밭 밑에 감춰진
강들의 서로 꼬인 수로들—

광활한 황야
　　외따른, 집.
황야 속의 그 작은 집.
　　그 집 속의 황야.

둘 다 잊혀진다.

　　　　무성

　　그 둘이 함께, 하나의 커다란 빈 집.

Riprap

Lay down these words
Before your mind like rocks.
  placed solid, by hands
In coice of place, set
Before the body of the mind
  in space and time:
Solidity of bark, leaf, or wall
  riprap of things:
Cobble of milky way,
  straying planets,
These poems, people,
  lost ponies with
Dragging saddles —
  and rocky sure-foot trails.
The worlds like an endless
  four-dimensional
Game of Go.
  ants and pebbles
In the thin loam, each rock a word
  a creek-washed stone
Granite: ingrained
  with torment of fire and weight
Crystal and sediment linked hot
  all change, in thoughts,
As well as things.

사석

네 마음 앞에 있는 이 말들을
돌처럼 깔아라
      단단하게, 손으로
좋은 곳에, 위치를 굳히는 데
마음의 몸 앞에
      시간과 공간 안에 :
단단한 나무껍질, 잎, 그리고 벽
      사물의 쇄석 :
은하수의 돌멩이,
      길잃은 위성들,
이 시들, 사람들,
      안장을 끌고 있는
길잃은 어린 말들
      그리고 바위같이 확실한 길들.
무한한 사차원의
      바둑시합 같은
세계들.
      개미들과 얇은 양토 속의
자갈들, 개개의 돌은 하나의 말
      냇물로 씻긴 돌
화강암 : 고뇌의 불과 무게로
      새겨졌고
수정과 앙금이 뜨겁게 연결되어
      모두 변한다, 생각에서,
사물에서처럼.

Song of the Taste

Eating the living germs of grasses
Eating the ova of large birds

    the fleshy sweetness packed
    around the sperm of swaying trees

The muscles of the flanks and thighs of
        soft-voiced cows
    the bounce in the lamb's leap
    the swish in the ox's tail

Eating roots grown swoll
        inside the soil

Drawing on life of living
    clustered points of light spun
        out of space
hidden in the grape.

Eating each other's seed
        eating
    ah, each other.

Kissing the lover in the mouth of bread:
        lip to lip.

미각의 모래

초목의 살아 있는 배종을 먹고
큰 새들의 알을 먹고

흔들리는 나무들의 정충 둘레에
저장한 과육질의 단맛

소리가 부드러운 소의
옆구리 허벅지 근육
뛰는 양의 탄력
쇠꼬리 휘두르는 소리

땅 속에서
크게 자란 뿌리를 먹고

우주에서
뽑아내어 포도에 숨겨져 있는
살아 있는 빛의 송이의 씨 안에서
생명을 끌어낸다.

서로 서로의 씨를 먹고
아, 서로를
먹는다.

연인인 빵의 입에 입맞춘다
입술에서 입술로.

Adrienne Rich (1929-2012)

Adrienne Rich was born in Baltimore, Maryland on May 16, 1929. She attended Radcliffe College, graduating in 1951, and was selected by W. H. Auden for the Yale Series of Younger Poets prize for *A Change of World* (1951) that same year.

In 1953, she married Harvard University economist Alfred H. Conrad. Two years later, she published her second volume of poetry, *The Diamond Cutters* (1955), of which Randall Jarrell wrote: "The poet [behind these poems] cannot help seeming to us a sort of princess in a fairy tale."

But the image of the fairytale princess would not be long-lived. After having three sons before the age of thirty, Rich gradually changed both her life and her poetry. Throughout the 1960s she wrote several collections, including *Snapshots of a Daughter-in-Law* (1963) and *Leaflets* (1969). The content of her work became increasingly confrontational—exploring such themes as women's role in society, racism, and the Vietnam War. The style of these poems also revealed a shift from careful metric patterns to free verse. In 1970, Rich left her husband, who committed suicide later that year.

It was in 1973, in the midst of the feminist and civil rights movements, the Vietnam War, and her own personal distress, that Rich wrote *Diving into the Wreck*, a collection of exploratory and often angry poems, which garnered her the National Book Award in 1974. Rich accepted the award on behalf of all women and shared it with her fellow nominees, Alice Walker and Audre Lorde.

About Rich's work, the poet W.S. Merwin has said, "All her life she has been in love with the hope of telling utter truth, and her command of language from the first has been startlingly powerful."

In 1997, she refused the National Medal of Arts, stating that "I could not accept such an award from President Clinton or this White House because the very meaning of art, as I understand it, is incompatible with the cynical politics of this administration." She went on to say: "[Art] means nothing if it simply decorates the dinner table of the power which holds it hostage."

The same year, Rich was awarded the Academy of American Poet's Wallace Stevens Award for outstanding and proven mastery in the art of poetry. She died on March 27, 2012, at the age of eighty-two.

Aunt Jennifer’s Tigers

Aunt Jennifer's tigers prance across a screen,
Bright topaz denizens of a world of green.
They do not fear the men beneath the tree;
They pace in sleek chivalric certainty.

Aunt Jennifer's finger fluttering through her wool
Find even the ivory needle hard to pull.
The massive weight of Uncle's wedding band
Sits heavily upon Aunt Jennifer's hand.

When Aunt is dead, her terrified hands will lie
Still ringed with ordeals she was mastered by.
The tigers in the panel that she made
Will go on prancing, proud and unafraid.

제니퍼 이모의 호랑이들

제니퍼 이모의 호랑이들이 의기양양하게 병풍 위를 가로지른다.
초록빛 세상 속 반짝이는 황옥색 동물들.
그들은 나무 밑 사냥꾼을 두려워하지 않는다.
그들은 늠름한 기사의 위세로 천천히 걷는다.

제니퍼 이모의 손가락이 털실 사이로 미세하게 떨린다.
상아 바늘을 끌어내는 것조차 힘겨워 보인다.
이모부가 준 결혼반지의 육중한 무게가
이모의 손가락을 묵직하게 누르고 있다.

이모가 돌아가실 때, 공포에 떨었던 그 두 손은 쉬게 될 것이다
그녀를 짓눌렀던 시련의 반지가 여전히 끼여 있겠지만.
이모가 수놓았던 병풍 속 호랑이들은
계속 활보할 것이다. 당당하게, 두려움 없이.

Implosions

The world's
not wanton
only wild and wavering

I wanted to choose words that even you
would have to be changed by

Take the word
of my pulse, loving and ordinary
Send out your signals, hoist
your dark scribbled flags
but take
my hand

All wars are useless to the dead

My hands are knotted in the rope
and I cannot sound the bell

My hands are frozen to the switch
and I cannot throw it

The foot is in the wheel

When it's finished and we're lying
in a stubble of blistered flowers
eyes gaping, mouths staring
dusted with crushed arterial blues

I'll have done nothing
even for you?

내파

세상은
썩어빠진 게 아니라
단지 난폭하게 요동치고 있을 뿐이에요.

당신조차 변화될 수밖에 없을
언어를 난 선택하고 싶었어요

내 맥박이 고동치는, 사랑스럽고 평범한
그 말을 받아들여요
당신의 신호를 보내요,
당신이 휘갈겨 쓴 검은 깃발을 게양해요
하지만 내 손을
잡아요

어떤 전쟁이든 죽은 이들에겐 소용없잖아요

내 두 손은 밧줄에 묶여 있어
종을 울릴 수 없어요

내 두 손은 스위치에 얼어붙어
그걸 던져버릴 수도 없어요

발은 바퀴살에 끼어 있어요

그게 끝나고 허리 꺾여 짓무른 꽃무더기에
으스러진 푸른 동맥혈 점점이 덮어쓰고
눈으로 숨을 쉬고, 입으로 바라보며
우리가 누워 있을 때

난 아무것도 한 게 없는 걸까요,
당신을 위해서조차?

Living in Sin

She had thought the studio would keep itself;
no dust upon the furniture of love.
Half heresy, to wish the taps less vocal,
the panes relieved of grime. A plate of pears,
a piano with a Persian shawl, a cat
stalking the picturesque amusing mouse
had risen at his urging.
Not that at five each separate stair would writhe
under the milkman's tramp; that morning light
so coldly would delineate the scraps
of last night's cheese and three sepulchral bottles;
that on the kitchen shelf among the saucers
a pair of beetle-eyes would fix her own—-
envoy from some village in the moldings . . .
Meanwhile, he, with a yawn,
sounded a dozen notes upon the keyboard,
declared it out of tune, shrugged at the mirror,
rubbed at his beard, went out for cigarettes;
while she, jeered by the minor demons,
pulled back the sheets and made the bed and found
a towel to dust the table-top,
and let the coffee-pot boil over on the stove.
By evening she was back in love again,
though not so wholly but throughout the night
she woke sometimes to feel the daylight coming
like a relentless milkman up the stairs.

죄의식 속에서 살기

그녀는 원룸 아파트가 잘 유지될 거라고,
사랑을 나눈 가구 위에는 먼지도 쌓이지 않을 거라고 생각했다.
반쯤 이단적이긴 해도, 수도꼭지에서 소리가 덜 날 거라고,
유리창이 기름때를 벗을 수 있을 거라고 소망했다.
배 한 접시, 페르시아산 숄이 걸쳐 있는 피아노,
만화에나 나올 법한 재밌게 생긴 쥐를 미행하다
그의 도발에 깜짝 놀라 튀어 올랐던 고양이[를 보면서].
문제는 다섯 시만 되면 우유배달부의 발걸음 아래서
계단이 삐걱거린다는 게 아니라, 아침 햇살이
어젯밤에 먹다 남은 치즈 조각이며 희뿌연 우유병 세 개를
너무도 냉정하게 보여준다는 거였다.
부엌 선반 위 접시 사이에서
딱정벌레의 두 눈이 그녀를 뚫어지게 쳐다보곤 했다—
선반 속 어떤 마을에서 온 대표 사절인 양……
한편, 그는, 하품을 하며,
열두 개의 건반을 눌러보고,
음정이 안 맞는다며, 거울 앞으로 가선 어깨를 으쓱해 보이고,
수염을 만지작거리더니, 담배를 사러 나갔다.
그동안 그녀는, 하찮은 악귀들에게 조롱당하며,
이불을 잘 펴고, 침대 정리를 하고,
탁자 위 먼지를 닦을 행주를 찾았다,
그리고 스토브 위에 커피 주전자를 놓고 물을 끓였다.
저녁 무렵 그녀는 그다지 완벽하지는 않았지만
다시 사랑을 했다, 밤새도록,
이따금 그녀는 잠이 깨어 새벽이 오는 것을 느꼈다.
마치 무정한 우유배달부가 계단을 올라오는 것처럼.

Power

Living in the earth-depositis of our history

Today a backhoe divulged out of a crumbling flank of earth
one bottle amber perfect a hundred-year-old
cure for fever or melancholy a tonic
for living on this earth in the winters of this climate

Today I was reading about Marie Curie:
she must have known she suffered from radiation sickness
her body bombarded for years by the element
she had purified
It seems she denied to the end
the source of the cataracts on her eyes
the cracked and suppurating skin of her finger-ends
till she could no longer hold a test-tube or a pencil

She died a famous woman denying
her wounds
denying
her wounds came from the same source as her power

힘

우리 역사의 땅속 저장소에 묻혀 산다는 것

오늘 부스러지는 흙더미 측면에서 굴착기가 공개하였다
열병 또는 우울증을 고칠
이런 겨울철 기후에 이 땅에서 살기 위해 필요한 물약이 담긴
백 년 된 호박색의 병 한 개를 온전한 상태로

오늘 나는 마리 퀴리의 전기를 읽고 있었다.
그녀는 틀림없이 자기가 아픈 것을 방사선 때문에 병이 생긴 것을
알고 있었을 것이다
자기가 정제했던 바로 그 요소 때문에 수년간 시달린 그녀의 육체
그녀의 두 눈에 생긴 백내장의 원인을
그녀의 손끝마다 피부가 갈라지고 고름이 나오는 원인을
시험 튜브나 연필조차 더 이상 들고 있을 수 없을 때까지
부인했던 것 같다

그녀는 상처를 부인하면서 아주 유명한 여인으로 죽었다
자신의 상처가
자신이 지닌 힘과 똑같은 원천에서 나왔다는 것을
부인하면서

Prospective Immigrants Please Note

Either you will
go through this door
or you will not go through.

If you go through
there is always the risk
of remembering your name.

Things look at you doubly
and you must look back
and let them happen.

If you do not go through
it is possible
to live worthily

to maintain your attitudes
to hold your position
to die bravely

but much will blind you,
much will evade you,
at what cost who knows?

The door itself makes no promises.
It is only a door.

장래의 이민자들을 위한 공지

당신은
이 문을 통과하든지
못하든지 할 것입니다.

만일 당신이 통과하더라도
당신의 이름을 기억하는
위험을 언제나 각오하십시오.

모든 것이 당신을 이중적으로 쳐다볼 것입니다
그러면 당신은 뒤를 돌아보고
그런 일이 일어나도록 내버려두십시오.

만일 당신이 통과하지 못하더라도
가치 있게 사는 것이
가능합니다

당신의 태도를 유지하면서
당신의 지위를 유지하면서
용감하게 죽는 것도요

하지만 많은 것이 당신을 장님으로 만들 것입니다,
많은 것이 당신을 스쳐 지나갈 것입니다,
어떤 비용을 치를지 누가 알겠습니까?

문 자체는 어떤 약속도 해주지 않습니다.
그것은 단지 문일 뿐이니까요.

Rape

There is a cop who is both prowler and father:
he comes from your block, grew up with your brothers,
had certain ideals.
You hardly know him in his boots and silver badge,
on horseback, one hand touching his gun.

You hardly know him but you have to get to know him:
he has access to machinery that could kill you.
He and his stallion clop like warlords among the trash,
his ideals stand in the air, a frozen cloud
from between his unsmiling lips.

And so, when the time comes, you have to turn to him,
the maniac's sperm still greasing your thighs,
your mind whirling like crazy. You have to confess
to him, you are guilty of the crime
of having been forced.

And you see his blue eyes, the blue eyes of all the family
whom you used to know, grow narrow and glisten,
his hand types out the details
and he wants them all
but the hysteria in your voice pleases him best.

You hardly know him but now he thinks he knows you:
he has taken down your worst moment
on a machine and filed it in a file.
He knows, or thinks he knows, how much you imagined;
he knows, or thinks he knows, what you secretly wanted.

강간

먹이를 찾아 헤매 다니는 사냥꾼이자 아빠인 경찰이 있다.
그는 같은 동네 출신이고, 당신의 형제들과 함께 어울려 자랐으며,
어떤 이상이란 것도 갖고 있다.
〔하지만〕 긴 부츠를 신고 은 배지를 달고 말 등에 올라타 한 손으로
총을 만지고 있는 그를 마주치면 잘 알아볼 수 없을 것이다.

그를 거의 알진 못하겠지만 그래도 당신은 그를 알아야만 한다.
그는 당신을 죽일 수 있는 총을 맘대로 가질 수 있다.
그는 말을 타고 군벌인 양 쓰레기 사이를 따각따각 지나간다,
그의 이상은 미소를 모르는 두 입술로 새 나오는 숨결의
얼어붙은 구름처럼 공기 중에 걸려 있다.

그러나, 때가 되면, 그에게 도움을 청해야 한다,
미친놈의 정액이 아직도 가랑이 사이로 흘러내리고,
정신이 아득해지고 미친 듯이 빙빙 돌 테니까. 그에게 고백해야 한다,
당신은 강간을 당한
죄를 졌으니까.

그리고 당신은 그가 파란 눈을, 당신이 가족처럼 친숙하게 보아왔던
그 파란 눈을, 가늘게 뜨고 반짝거리며,
두 손으로 자세한 사항을 타이프로 치고 있는 것을 본다
그는 모든 것을 상세하게 알고 싶어 하지만,
그를 가장 즐겁게 하는 것은 겁에 질려 흥분한 당신의 목소리이다.

당신은 그를 거의 알지 못하지만, 그는 이제 당신을 잘 안다고 여긴다.
그는 당신 인생에서 가장 괴로운 순간을 타이프로 쳐서
서류로 만든 뒤, 그것을 서류 정리함에 집어넣는다.
그는 안다, 혹은 안다고 생각한다,
당신이 얼마나 많이 그런 상상을 했는지를.
그는 안다, 혹은 안다고 생각한다, 당신이 남몰래 무어을 원했던지를.

He has access to machinery that could get you put away;
and if, in the sickening light of the precinct,
and if, in the sickening light of the precinct,
your details sound like a portrait of your confessor,
will you swallow, will you deny them, will you lie your way home?

그는 당신을 보내버릴 수 있는 기계 같은 조직에 마음대로 접근할 수
있다.
그리고 만약, 경찰서의 구역질 나는 불빛 속에서,
그리고 만약, 경찰서의 구역질 나는 불빛 속에서,
당신이 말한 자세한 사항이 당신의 고해신부의 모습을 그려낸다면
당신은 수치심을 삼키며 그 사실을 부인할 것인가, 거짓말을 하고
집으로 돌아갈 것인가?

최동오

문학과환경학회 회장 역임
현 충남대학교 영어영문학과 교수

낭만주의 영시, 현대 영미시, 생태문학을 가르침.
저서로는 『영어권 생태문학의 현황』이 있고
공저로는 『인지문화란 무엇인가』 등이 있음.
논문으로는 「낭만시와 박물학적 상상력」 외 다수 있음.

현대 영미시의 이해

초판 발행 _ 2019년 8월 30일

편 저 자 • 최 동 오
발 행 인 • 정 현 걸
발 행 • 신 아 사
인 쇄 • 현대문화사
주 소 • 서울시 은평구 통일로 59길 4(2F)
전 화 • 02)382-6411 · 팩스 02)382-6401
홈페이지 • www.shinasa.co.kr
E-MAIL • shinasa@daum.net
출판등록 • 1956년 1월 5일 (제9-52호)

ISBN 978-89-8396-364-2(93840)

정가 14,000원